PENGUIN BOOKS — GREAT IDEAS

Human Happiness

Blaise Pascal
1623–1662

Blaise Pascal

Human Happiness

TRANSLATED BY A. J. KRAILSHEIMER

PENGUIN BOOKS — GREAT IDEAS

PENGUIN BOOKS

Published by the Penguin Group
Penguin Books Ltd, 80 Strand, London WC2R ORL, England
Penguin Group (USA) Inc., 375 Hudson Street, New York, New York 10014, USA
Penguin Group (Canada), 90 Eglinton Avenue East, Suite 700, Toronto, Ontario, Canada M4P 2Y3
(a division of Pearson Penguin Canada Inc.)
Penguin Ireland, 25 St Stephen's Green, Dublin 2, Ireland
(a division of Penguin Books Ltd)
Penguin Group (Australia), 250 Camberwell Road, Camberwell, Victoria 3124, Australia
(a division of Pearson Australia Group Pty Ltd)
Penguin Books India Pvt Ltd, 11 Community Centre, Panchsheel Park, New Delhi – 110 017, India
Penguin Group (NZ), 67 Apollo Drive, Rosedale, North Shore 0632, New Zealand
(a division of Pearson New Zealand Ltd)
Penguin Books (South Africa) (Pty) Ltd, 24 Sturdee Avenue,
Rosebank, Johannesburg 2196, South Africa

Penguin Books Ltd, Registered Offices: 80 Strand, London WC2R ORL, England

www.penguin.com

This translation first published as a Penguin Classic 1966
Revised edition first published 1995
This selection first published 2008

014

Translation © A. J. Krailsheimer 1966, 1995

Set by Rowland Phototypesetting Ltd, Bury St Edmunds, Suffolk

Printed and bound in Great Britain by Clays Ltd, Elcograf S.p.A.

978-0-141-03679-3

www.greenpenguin.co.uk

MIX
Paper | Supporting
responsible forestry
FSC® C018072

Penguin Books is committed to a sustainable
future for our business, our readers and our planet.
This book is made from Forest Stewardship
Council™ certified paper.

In this selection of extracts the numbering system for the individual pensées is that used in the Penguin Classics edition.

21 If we are too young our judgement is impaired, just as it is if we are too old.

Thinking too little about things or thinking too much both make us obstinate and fanatical.

If we look at our work immediately after completing it, we are still too involved; if too long afterwards, we cannot pick up the thread again.

It is like looking at pictures which are too near or too far away. There is just one indivisible point which is the right place.

Others are too near, too far, too high, or too low. In painting the rules of perspective decide it, but how will it be decided when it comes to truth and morality?

22 Flies are so mighty that they win battles, paralyse our minds, eat up our bodies.

23 *Vanity of science.* Knowledge of physical science will not console me for ignorance of morality in time of affliction, but knowledge of morality will always console me for ignorance of physical science.

24 *Man's condition.* Inconstancy, boredom, anxiety.

25 The fact that kings are habitually seen in the company of guards, drums, officers and all the things

which prompt automatic responses of respect and fear has the result that, when they are sometimes alone and unaccompanied, their features are enough to strike respect and fear into their subjects, because we make no mental distinction between their person and the retinue with which they are normally seen to be associated. And the world, which does not know that this is the effect of habit, believes it to derive from some natural force, hence such sayings as: 'The character of divinity is stamped on his features.'

26 The power of kings is founded on the reason and the folly of the people, but especially on their folly. The greatest and most important thing in the world is founded on weakness. This is a remarkably sure foundation, for nothing is surer than that the people will be weak. Anything founded on sound reason is very ill-founded, like respect for wisdom.

30 We do not choose as captain of a ship the most highly born of those aboard.

31 We do not care about our reputation in towns where we are only passing through. But when we have to stay some time we do care. How much time does it take? A time proportionate to our vain and paltry existence.

33 What amazes me most is to see that everyone is not amazed at his own weakness. We behave seriously, and everyone follows his calling, not because it is really a good thing to do so, in accord-

ance with fashion, but as if everyone knew for certain where reason and justice lie. We are constantly disappointed and an absurd humility makes us blame ourselves and not the skill we always boast of having. But it is a good thing for the reputation of scepticism that there are so many people about who are not sceptics, to show that man is quite capable of the most extravagant opinions, since he is capable of believing that he is not naturally and inevitably weak, but is, on the contrary, naturally wise.

36 Anyone who does not see the vanity of the world is very vain himself. So who does not see it, apart from young people whose lives are all noise, diversions, and thoughts for the future?

But take away their diversion and you will see them bored to extinction. Then they feel their nullity without recognizing it, for nothing could be more wretched than to be intolerably depressed as soon as one is reduced to introspection with no means of diversion.

42 How many kingdoms know nothing of us!

43 A trifle consoles us because a trifle upsets us.

44 *Imagination*. It is the dominant faculty in man, master of error and falsehood, all the more deceptive for not being invariably so; for it would be an infallible criterion of truth if it were infallibly that of lies. Since, however, it is usually false, it gives no indication of its quality, setting the same mark on true and false alike.

I am not speaking of fools, but of the wisest men, amongst whom imagination is best entitled to persuade. Reason may object in vain, it cannot fix the price of things.

This arrogant force, which checks and dominates its enemy, reason, for the pleasure of showing off the power it has in every sphere, has established a second nature in man. Imagination has its happy and unhappy men, its sick and well, its rich and poor; it makes us believe, doubt, deny reason; it deadens the senses, it arouses them; it has its fools and sages, and nothing annoys us more than to see it satisfy its guests more fully and completely than reason ever could. Those who are clever in imagination are far more pleased with themselves than prudent men could reasonably be. They look down on people with a lofty air; they are bold and confident in argument, where others are timid and unsure, and their cheerful demeanour often wins the verdict of their listeners, for those whose wisdom is imaginary enjoy the favour of judges similarly qualified. Imagination cannot make fools wise, but it makes them happy, as against reason, which only makes its friends wretched: one covers them with glory, the other with shame.

Who dispenses reputation? Who makes us respect and revere persons, works, laws, the great? Who but this faculty of imagination? All the riches of the earth are inadequate without its approval. Would you not say that this magistrate, whose venerable age commands universal respect, is ruled by pure, sublime reason, and judges things as they really are, without paying heed to the trivial circumstances which offend only the imagination of weaker men? See him go to hear a sermon in a spirit of pious zeal, the soundness of his judgement strengthened by the ardour of his charity, ready to listen with exemplary respect. If, when the preacher appears, it turns out that nature has given him a hoarse voice and an odd sort of face, that his barber has shaved him badly and he happens not to be too clean either, then, whatever great truths he may announce, I wager that our senator will not be able to keep a straight face.

Put the world's greatest philosopher on a plank that is wider than need be: if there is a precipice below, although his reason may convince him that he is safe, his imagination will prevail. Many could not even stand the thought of it without going pale and breaking into sweat.

I do not intend to list all the effects of imagination. Everyone knows that the sight of cats, or rats, the crunching of a coal, etc., is enough to unhinge reason. The tone of voice influences the wisest of us and alters the force of a speech or a poem.

Love or hate alters the face of justice. An advocate who has been well paid in advance will find the cause he is pleading all the more just. The boldness of his bearing will make it seem all the better to the judges, taken in by appearances. How absurd is reason, the sport of every wind! I should list almost all the actions of men, who hardly stir except when jolted by imagination. For reason has had to yield, and at its wisest adopts those principles which human imagination has rashly introduced at every turn. Anyone who chose to follow reason alone would have proved himself a fool. We must, since reason so pleases, work all day for benefits recognized as imaginary, and, when sleep has refreshed us from the toils of our reason, we must at once jump up to pursue the phantoms and endure the impressions created by this ruler of the world. Here is one of the principles of error, but not the only one.

Man has been quite right to make these two powers into allies, although in this peace imagination enjoys an extensive advantage; for in conflict its advantage is more complete. Reason never wholly overcomes imagination, while the contrary is quite common.

Our magistrates have shown themselves well aware of this mystery. Their red robes, the ermine in which they swaddle themselves like furry cats, the law-courts where they sit in judgement, the fleurs de lys, all this august panoply was very necessary. If physicians did not have long gowns and mules, if learned doctors did not wear square caps and robes four times too large, they would never have deceived the world, which finds such an authentic display irresistible. If they possessed true justice, and if physicians possessed the true art of healing, they would not need square caps; the majesty of such sciences would command respect in itself. But, as they only possess imaginary science, they have to resort to these vain devices in order to strike the imagination, which is their real concern, and this, in fact, is how they win respect.

Soldiers are the only ones who do not disguise themselves in this way, because their role is really more essential; they establish themselves by force, the others by masquerade.

That is why our kings have not attempted to disguise themselves. They have not dressed up in extraordinary clothes to show what they are, but they have themselves escorted by guards, scarred veterans. These armed troops whose hands and strength are theirs alone, the drums and trumpets that march before them, and these legions which surround them make the most resolute tremble. They do not wear the trappings, they simply have the power. It would take reason at its most refined to see the Grand Turk, surrounded in his superb seraglio by 40,000 janissaries, as a man like any other.

We have only to see a lawyer in cap and gown to form a favourable opinion of his competence.

Imagination decides everything: it creates beauty, justice and happiness, which is the world's supreme good. I should dearly like to see the Italian book, of which I know only the title, worth many books in itself, *Dell'opinione regina del mondo*. Without knowing the book, I support its views, apart from any evil it may contain.

Such, more or less, are the effects of this deceptive faculty, apparently given to us for the specific purpose of leading us inevitably into error. We have plenty of other principles of error.

Longstanding impressions are not the only ones that can mislead us; the charms of novelty have the same power. Hence all the debate among men, who accuse each other either of following the false impressions of childhood or of rashly pursuing new ones. If anyone has found the golden mean, let him appear and prove it. Any principle, however natural it may be, even implanted in childhood, may be treated as a false impression either of education or of the senses.

'Because,' they say, 'you have believed since you were a child that a box was empty when you could not see anything in it, you believed that a vacuum could exist. This is just an illusion of your senses, strengthened by habit, and it must be corrected by science.' Others say: 'When you were taught at school that there is no such thing as a vacuum, your common sense was corrupted; it was quite clear about it before being given the wrong impression, and now it must be corrected by reverting to your original state.' Who then is the deceiver, the senses or education?

We have another principle of error in illnesses, which impair our judgement and sense. If serious illnesses do considerable harm, I have no doubt that the less serious ones have a proportionate effect.

Our own interest is another wonderful instrument for blinding us agreeably. The fairest man in the world is not allowed to be judge in his own cause. I know of men who, to avoid the danger of partiality in their own favour, have leaned over to the opposite extreme of injustice. The surest way to lose a perfectly just case was to get close relatives to commend it to them. Justice and truths are two points so fine that our instruments are too blunt to touch them exactly. If they do make contact, they blunt the point and press all round on the false rather than the true.

Man, then, is so happily constituted that he has no exact principle of truth, and several excellent ones of falsehood. Let us now see how many.

But the most absurd cause of his errors is the war between the senses and the reason.

46 *Vanity.* The cause and effect of love. Cleopatra.

47 We never keep to the present. We recall the past; we anticipate the future as if we found it too slow in coming and were trying to hurry it up, or we recall the past as if to stay its too rapid flight. We are so unwise that we wander about in times that do not belong to us, and do not think of the only one that does; so vain that we dream of times that are not and blindly flee the only one that is. The fact is that the present usually hurts. We thrust it out of sight because it distresses us, and if we find it enjoyable, we are sorry to see it slip away. We try to give it the support of the future, and think how we are going to arrange things over which we have no control for a time we can never be sure of reaching.

Let each of us examine his thoughts; he will find them wholly concerned with the past or the future. We almost never think of the present, and if we do think of it, it is only to see what light it throws on our plans for the future. The present is never our end. The past and the present are our means, the future alone our end. Thus we never actually live, but hope to live, and since we are always planning how to be happy, it is inevitable that we should never be so.

49 Caesar was too old, it seems to me, to go off and amuse himself conquering the world. Such a pastime was all right for Augustus and Alexander; they were young men, not easily held in check, but Caesar ought to have been more mature.

53 Man is vile enough to bow down to beasts and even worship them.

54 *Inconstancy*. Things have various qualities and the soul various tendencies, for nothing presented to the soul is simple, and the soul never applies itself simply to any subject. That is why the same thing makes us laugh and cry.

55 *Inconstancy*. We think playing upon man is like playing upon an ordinary organ. It is indeed an organ, but strange, shifting and changeable. Those who only know how to play an ordinary organ would never be in tune on this one. You have to know where the keys are.

56 We are so unhappy that we can only enjoy something which we should be annoyed to see go wrong, and that can and does constantly happen to thousands of things. Anyone who found the secret of rejoicing when things go well without being annoyed when they go badly would have found the point. It is perpetual motion.

57 It is not good to be too free.
It is not good to have all one needs.

58 Tyranny consists in the desire to dominate everything regardless of order.

In the various departments for men of strength, beauty, sense and piety, each man is master in his own house but nowhere else. Sometimes they meet and the strong and the handsome contend for mastery, but this is idiotic because their mastery is of different kinds. They do not understand each other and their mistake lies in wanting to rule everywhere. Nothing can do that, not even strength: it is of no effect in the learned world and only governs external actions. – So these arguments are false . . .

Tyranny. Tyranny is wanting to have by one means what can only be had by another. We pay different dues to different kinds of merit; we must love charm, fear strength, believe in knowledge.

These dues must be paid. It is wrong to refuse them and wrong to demand any others. So these arguments are false and tyrannical: 'I am handsome, so you must fear me. I am strong, so you must love me, I am . . .' In the same way it is false and tyrannical to say: 'He is not strong, so I will not respect him. He is not clever, so I will not fear him.'

65 *Diversity*. Theology is a science, but at the same time how many sciences? A man is a substance, but if you dissect him, what is he? Head, heart, stomach, veins, each vein, each bit of vein, blood, each humour of blood?

A town or a landscape from afar off is a town and a landscape, but as one approaches it becomes houses, trees, tiles, leaves, grass, ants, ants' legs, and so on *ad infinitum*. All that is comprehended in the word 'landscape'.

68 When I consider the brief span of my life absorbed into the eternity which comes before and after – *as the remembrance of a guest that tarrieth but a day* – the small space I occupy and which I see swallowed up in the infinite immensity of spaces of which I know nothing and which know nothing of me, I take fright and am amazed to see myself here rather than there: there is no reason for me to be here rather than there, now rather than then. Who put me here? By whose command and act were this time and place allotted to me?

69 *Wretchedness*. Job and Solomon.

70 If our condition were truly happy we should not need to divert ourselves from thinking about it.

71 *Contradictions*. Pride counterbalances all these miseries; man either hides or displays them, and glories in his awareness of them.

72 One must know oneself. Even if that does not help in finding truth, at least it helps in running one's life, and nothing is more proper.

73 What causes inconstancy is the realization that present pleasures are false, together with the failure to realize that absent pleasures are vain.

77 *Pride*. Curiosity is only vanity. We usually only want to know something so that we can talk about it; in other words, we would never travel by sea if it meant never talking about it, and for the sheer pleasure of seeing things we could never hope to describe to others.

78 *Description of man*. Dependence, desire for independence, needs.

79 How tiresome it is to give up pursuits to which we have become attached. A man enjoying a happy home-life has only to see a woman who attracts him, or spend five or six pleasant days gambling, and he will be very sorry to go back to what he was doing before. It happens every day.

80 Respect means: put yourself out. That may look pointless, but it is quite right, because it amounts to saying: I should certainly put myself out if you needed it, because I do so when you do not; besides, respect serves to distinguish the great. If respect

meant sitting in an armchair we should be showing everyone respect and then there would be no way of marking distinction, but we make the distinction quite clear by putting ourselves out.

81 The only universal rules are the law of the land in everyday matters and the will of the majority in others. How is that? Because of the power implied.

That is why kings, who have another source of power, do not follow the majority of their ministers.

Equality of possessions is no doubt right, but, as men could not make might obey right, they have made right obey might. As they could not fortify justice they have justified force, so that right and might live together and peace reigns, the sovereign good.

82 Wisdom leads us back to childhood. *Except ye become as little children.*

83 The world is a good judge of things, because it is in the state of natural ignorance where man really belongs. Knowledge has two extremes which meet; one is the pure natural ignorance of every man at birth, the other is the extreme reached by great minds who run through the whole range of human knowledge, only to find that they know nothing and come back to the same ignorance from which they set out, but it is a wise ignorance which knows itself. Those who stand half-way have put their natural ignorance behind them without yet attaining the other; they have some smattering of

adequate knowledge and pretend to understand everything. They upset the world and get everything wrong.

Ordinary people and clever people make up the run of the world; the former despise it and are despised in their turn. All their judgements are wrong and the world judges them rightly.

84 *Descartes*. In general terms one must say: 'That is the result of figure and motion,' because it is true, but to name them and assemble the machine is quite ridiculous. It is pointless, uncertain, and arduous. Even if it were true we do not think that the whole of philosophy would be worth an hour's effort.

86 *Of true justice*. We no longer have any. If we had, we should not accept it as a rule of justice that one should follow the customs of one's country.

That is why we have found might when we could not find right.

87 The chancellor is a grave man, dressed in fine robes because his position is false; not so the king. He enjoys power, and has no use for imagination. Judges, doctors, etc., enjoy nothing but imagination.

88 It is the effect of power, not of custom, for those capable of originality are rare. Those who are strongest in numbers only want to follow, and refuse recognition to those who seek it for their originality. If they persist in wanting recognition and despising those who are not original, the others will call them

ridiculous names and may even beat them. So do not be conceited about your subtlety, or keep your satisfaction to yourself.

94 *Sound opinions of the people*. The greatest of evils is civil war.

It is bound to come if people want to reward merit, because everyone will claim to be meritorious. The evil to be feared if the succession falls by right of birth to a fool is neither so great nor so certain.

95 *Sound opinions of the people*. It is not mere vanity to be elegant, because it shows that a lot of people are working for you. Your hair shows that you have a valet, a perfumer, etc., bands, thread, braid, etc., show . . . It means more than superficial show or mere accoutrement to have many hands in one's service.

The more hands one employs the more powerful one is. Elegance is a means of showing one's power.

98 How is it that a lame man does not annoy us while a lame mind does? Because a lame man recognizes that we are walking straight, while a lame mind says that it is we who are limping. But for that we should feel sorry rather than angry.

Epictetus goes much further when he asks: Why do we not lose our temper if someone tells us that we have a headache, while we do lose it if someone says there is anything wrong with our arguments or our choice?

99 The reason for that is that we are quite certain that we have not got a headache, and are not limping, but we are not so sure we are making the right choice. Consequently, since the only thing that makes us sure is the evidence available to us, we hesitate and are taken aback when the evidence available to someone else makes him see just the opposite. All the more so when a thousand other people scoff at our choice, because we are obliged to prefer our judgement to that of so many others, and that is a bold and difficult thing to do. There is never such a clash of views over a lame man.

Man is so made that if he is told often enough that he is a fool he believes it. By telling himself so often enough he convinces himself, because when he is alone he carries on an inner dialogue with himself which it is important to keep under proper control. *Evil communications corrupt good manners.* We must keep silence as far as we can and only talk to ourselves about God, whom we know to be true, and thus convince ourselves that he is.

103 *Right, might.* It is right to follow the right, it is necessary to follow the mighty.

Right without might is helpless, might without right is tyrannical.

Right without might is challenged, because there are always evil men about. Might without right is denounced. We must therefore combine right and might, and to that end make right into might or might into right.

Right is open to dispute, might is easily recognized and beyond dispute. Therefore right could not be made mighty because might challenged right, calling it unjust and itself claiming to be just.

Being thus unable to make right into might, we have made might into right.

104 What a great advantage to be of noble birth, since it gives a man of eighteen the standing, recognition and respect that another man might not earn before he was fifty. That means winning thirty years' start with no effort.

105 If an animal did rationally what it does by instinct, and if it spoke rationally what it speaks by instinct when hunting, or warning its fellows that the prey has been lost or found, it would certainly go on to talk about matters which affect it more seriously, and it would say, for instance: 'Bite through this cord; it is hurting me and I cannot reach it.'

106 *Greatness.* Causes and effects show the greatness of man in producing such excellent order from his own concupiscence.

107 The parrot wipes its beak although it is clean.

108 What part of us feels pleasure? Is it our hand, our arm, our flesh, or our blood? It must obviously be something immaterial.

109 *Against Scepticism.* It is odd that we cannot define these things without making them obscure; we talk about them all the time. We assume that everyone

conceives of them in the same way, but that it is a quite gratuitous assumption, because we have no proof that it is so. I see indeed that we apply these words on the same occasions; every time two men see a body change its position they both use the same word to express what they have seen, each of them saying that the body has moved. Such conformity of application provides a strong presumption of conformity of thought, but it lacks the absolute force of total conviction, although the odds are that it is so, because we know that the same conclusions are often drawn from different assumptions.

That is enough to cloud the issue, to say the least, though it does not completely extinguish the natural light which provides us with certainty in such matters. The Platonists would have wagered on it, but that makes the light dimmer and upsets the dogmatists, to the glory of the sceptical clique which stands for ambiguous ambiguity, and a certain dubious obscurity from which our doubts cannot remove every bit of light any more than our natural light can dispel all the darkness.

110 We know the truth not only through our reason but also through our heart. It is through the latter that we know first principles, and reason, which has nothing to do with it, tries in vain to refute them. The sceptics have no other object than that, and they work at it to no purpose. We know that we are not dreaming, but, however unable we may be

to prove it rationally, our inability proves nothing but the weakness of our reason, and not the uncertainty of all our knowledge, as they maintain. For knowledge of first principles, like space, time, motion, number, is as solid as any derived through reason, and it is on such knowledge, coming from the heart and instinct, that reason has to depend and base all its argument. The heart feels that there are three spatial dimensions and that there is an infinite series of numbers, and reason goes on to demonstrate that there are no two square numbers of which one is double the other. Principles are felt, propositions proved, and both with certainty though by different means. It is just as pointless and absurd for reason to demand proof of first principles from the heart before agreeing to accept them as it would be absurd for the heart to demand an intuition of all the propositions demonstrated by reason before agreeing to accept them.

Our inability must therefore serve only to humble reason, which would like to be the judge of everything, but not to confute our certainty. As if reason were the only way we could learn! Would to God, on the contrary, that we never needed it and knew everything by instinct and feeling! But nature has refused us this blessing, and has instead given us only very little knowledge of this kind; all other knowledge can be acquired only by reasoning.

That is why those to whom God has given religious faith by moving their hearts are very fortunate, and feel quite legitimately convinced, but to those who do not have it we can only give such faith through reasoning, until God gives it by moving their heart, without which faith is only human and useless for salvation.

111 I can certainly imagine a man without hands, feet, or head, for it is only experience that teaches us that the head is more necessary than the feet. But I cannot imagine a man without thought; he would be a stone or an animal.

112 Instinct and reason, signs of two natures.

113 *Thinking reed.* It is not in space that I must seek my human dignity, but in the ordering of my thought. It will do me no good to own land. Through space the universe grasps me and swallows me up like a speck; through thought I grasp it.

114 Man's greatness comes from knowing he is wretched: a tree does not know it is wretched.

Thus it is wretched to know that one is wretched, but there is greatness in knowing one is wretched.

115 *Immateriality of the soul.* When philosophers have subdued their passions, what material substance has managed to achieve this?

116 All these examples of wretchedness prove his greatness. It is the wretchedness of a great lord, the wretchedness of a dispossessed king.

117 *Man's greatness.* Man's greatness is so obvious that it can even be deduced from his wretchedness, for

what is nature in animals we call wretchedness in man, thus recognizing that, if his nature is today like that of the animals, he must have fallen from some better state which was once his own.

Who indeed would think himself unhappy not to be king except one who had been dispossessed? Did anyone think Paulus Emilius was unhappy not to be consul? On the contrary, everyone thought he was happy to have been so once, because the office was not meant to be permanent. But people thought Perseus so unhappy at finding himself no longer king, because that was meant to be a permanent office, that they were surprised that he could bear to go on living. Who would think himself unhappy if he had only one mouth and who would not if he had only one eye? It has probably never occurred to anyone to be distressed at not having three eyes, but those who have none are inconsolable.

118 Man's greatness even in his concupiscence. He has managed to produce such a remarkable system from it and make it the image of true charity.

119 *Contradictions.* (After showing how vile and how great man is.) Let man now judge his own worth, let him love himself, for there is within him a nature capable of good; but that is no reason for him to love the vileness within himself. Let him despise himself because this capacity remains unfilled; but that is no reason for him to despise this natural capacity. Let him both hate and love himself; he

has within him the capacity for knowing truth and being happy, but he possesses no truth which is either abiding or satisfactory.

I should therefore like to arouse in man the desire to find truth, to be ready, free from passion, to follow it wherever he may find it, realizing how far his knowledge is clouded by passions. I should like him to hate his concupiscence which automatically makes his decisions for him, so that it should not blind him when he makes his choice, nor hinder him once he has chosen.

120 We are so presumptuous that we should like to be known all over the world, even by people who will only come when we are no more. Such is our vanity that the good opinion of half a dozen of the people around us gives us pleasure and satisfaction.

121 It is dangerous to explain too clearly to man how like he is to the animals without pointing out his greatness. It is also dangerous to make too much of his greatness without his vileness. It is still more dangerous to leave him in ignorance of both, but it is most valuable to represent both to him.

Man must not be allowed to believe that he is equal either to animals or to angels, nor to be unaware of either, but he must know both.

122 *Greatness and wretchedness.* Since wretchedness and greatness can be concluded each from the other, some people have been more inclined to conclude that man is wretched for having used his greatness

to prove it, while others have all the more cogently concluded he is great by basing their proof on wretchedness. Everything that could be said by one side as proof of greatness has only served as an argument for the others to conclude he is wretched, since the further one falls the more wretched one is, and vice versa. One has followed the other in an endless circle, for it is certain that as man's insight increases so he finds both wretchedness and greatness within himself. In a word man knows he is wretched. Thus he is wretched because he is so, but he is truly great because he knows it.

123 *Contradictions*. Contempt for our existence, dying for nothing, hatred of our existence.

124 *Contradictions*. Man is naturally credulous, incredulous, timid, bold.

125 What are our natural principles but habitual principles? In children it is the principles received from the habits of their fathers, like hunting in the case of animals.

A change of habit will produce different natural principles, as can be seen from experience, and if there are some principles which habit cannot eradicate, there are others both habitual and unnatural which neither nature nor a new habit can eradicate. It all depends on one's disposition.

126 Fathers are afraid that their children's natural love may be eradicated. What then is this nature which is liable to be eradicated?

Habit is a second nature that destroys the first. But what is nature? Why is habit not natural? I am very much afraid that nature itself is only a first habit, just as habit is a second nature.

127 Man's nature may be considered in two ways; either according to his end, and then he is great and beyond compare, or according to the masses, as the nature of horses and dogs is judged by the masses from seeing how they run or ward off strangers, and then man is abject and vile. These are the two approaches which provoke such divergent views and such argument among philosophers, because each denies the other's hypothesis.

One says: 'Man was not born for this end, because everything he does belies it.' The other says: 'He is falling far short of his end when he acts so basely.'

128 Two things teach man about his whole nature: instinct and experience.

129 *Trade. Thoughts.* All is one, all is diversity.

How many natures lie in human nature! How many occupations! How fortuitously in the ordinary way each of us takes up the one that he has heard others praise. A well-turned heel.

130 If he exalts himself, I humble him.

If he humbles himself, I exalt him.

And I go on contradicting him

Until he understands

That he is a monster that passes all understanding.

131 The strongest of the sceptics' arguments, to say nothing of minor points, is that we cannot be sure that these principles are true (faith and revelation apart) except through some natural intuition. Now this natural intuition affords no convincing proof that they are true. There is no certainty, apart from faith, as to whether man was created by a good God, an evil demon, or just by chance, and so it is a matter of doubt, depending on our origin, whether these innate principles are true, false or uncertain.

Moreover, no one can be sure, apart from faith, whether he is sleeping or waking, because when we are asleep we are just as firmly convinced that we are awake as we are now. As we often dream we are dreaming, piling up one dream on another, is it not possible that this half of our life is itself just a dream, on to which the others are grafted, and from which we shall awake when we die? That while it lasts we are as little in possession of the principles of truth and goodness as during normal sleep? All this passage of time, of life, all these different bodies which we feel, the different thoughts which stir us, may be no more than illusions like the passage of time and vain phantoms of our dreams. We think we are seeing space, shape, movement, we feel time pass, we measure it, in fact we behave just as we do when we are awake. As a result, since half our life is spent in sleep, on our own admission and despite appearances we have no idea of the truth because all our intuitions are simply illusions during that time. Who knows whether the other half of our lives, when we think we are awake, is not another sleep slightly different from the first, on to which our dreams are grafted as our sleep appears, and from which we awake when we think we are sleeping? And who can doubt that, if we dreamed in the company of others and our dreams happened to agree, which is common enough, and if we were alone when awake, we should think things had been turned upside-down?

These are the main points on each side, to say nothing of minor arguments, like those the sceptics direct against the influences of habit, education, local customs, and so on, which the slightest puff of scepticism overturns, though they convince the majority of ordinary people, who have only this vain basis for their dogmas. You have only to look at their books; if you are not sufficiently persuaded you soon will be, perhaps too much so.

I pause at the dogmatists' only strong point, which is that we cannot doubt natural principles if we speak sincerely and in all good faith.

To which the sceptics reply, in a word, that uncertainty as to our origin entails uncertainty as to our nature. The dogmatists have been trying to answer that ever since the world began.

(Anyone wanting ampler information about scepticism should look at their books; he will soon be persuaded, perhaps too much so.)

This means open war between men, in which everyone is obliged to take sides, either with the dogmatists or with the sceptics, because anyone who imagines he can stay neutral is a sceptic *par excellence*. This neutrality is the essence of their clique. Anyone who is not against them is their staunch supporter, and that is where their advantage appears. They are not even for themselves; they are neutral, indifferent, suspending judgment on everything, including themselves.

What then is man to do in this state of affairs? Is he to doubt everything, to doubt whether he is awake, whether he is being pinched or burned? Is he to doubt whether he is doubting, to doubt whether he exists?

No one can go that far, and I maintain that a perfectly genuine sceptic has never existed. Nature backs up helpless reason and stops it going so wildly astray.

Is he, on the other hand, to say that he is the certain possessor of truth, when at the slightest pressure he fails to prove his claim and is compelled to loose his grasp?

What sort of freak then is man! How novel, how monstrous, how chaotic, how paradoxical, how prodigious! Judge of all things, feeble earthworm, repository of truth, sink of doubt and error, glory and refuse of the universe!

Who will unravel such a tangle? This is certainly beyond dogmatism and scepticism, beyond all human philosophy. Man transcends man. Let us then concede to the sceptics what they have so often proclaimed, that truth lies beyond our scope and is an unattainable quarry, that it is no earthly denizen, but at home in heaven, lying in the lap of God, to be known only in so far as it pleases him to reveal it. Let us learn our true nature from the uncreated and incarnate truth.

If we seek truth through reason we cannot avoid one of these three sects. You cannot be a sceptic or a Platonist without stifling nature, you cannot be a dogmatist without turning your back on reason.

Nature confounds the sceptics and Platonists, and reason confounds the dogmatists. What then will become of you, man, seeking to discover your true condition through natural reason? You cannot avoid one of these three sects nor survive in any of them.

Know then, proud man, what a paradox you are to yourself. Be humble, impotent reason! Be silent, feeble nature! Learn that man infinitely transcends man, hear from your master your true condition, which is unknown to you.

Listen to God.

Is it not as clear as day that man's condition is dual? The point is that if man had never been corrupted, he would, in his innocence, confidently enjoy both truth and felicity, and, if man had never been anything but corrupt, he would have no idea either of truth or bliss. But unhappy as we are (and we should be less so if there were no element of greatness in our condition) we have an idea of happiness but we cannot attain it. We perceive an image of the truth and possess nothing but falsehood, being equally incapable of absolute ignorance and certain knowledge; so obvious is it that we once enjoyed a degree of perfection from which we have unhappily fallen.

Let us then conceive that man's condition is dual. Let us conceive that man infinitely transcends man, and that without the aid of faith he would remain inconceivable to himself, for who cannot see that unless we realize the duality of human nature we remain invincibly ignorant of the truth about ourselves?

It is, however, an astounding thing that the mystery furthest from our ken, that of the transmission of sin, should be something without which we can have no knowledge of ourselves.

Without doubt nothing is more shocking to our reason than to say that the sin of the first man has implicated in its guilt men so far from the original sin that they seem incapable of sharing it. This flow of guilt does not seem merely impossible to us, but indeed most unjust. What could be more contrary to the rules of our miserable justice than the eternal damnation of a child, incapable of will, for an act in which he seems to have so little part that it was actually committed 6,000 years before he existed? Certainly nothing jolts us more rudely than this doctrine, and yet, but for this mystery, the most incomprehensible of all, we remain incomprehensible to ourselves. The knot of our condition was twisted and turned in that abyss, so that it is harder to conceive of man without this mystery than for man to conceive of it himself.

This shows that God, in his desire to make the

difficulties of our existence unintelligible to us, hid the knot so high, or more precisely, so low, that we were quite unable to reach it. Consequently it is not through the proud activity of our reason but through its simple submission that we can really know ourselves.

These fundamental facts, solidly established on the inviolable authority of religion, teach us that there are in faith two equally constant truths. One is that man in the state of his creation, or in the state of grace, is exalted above the whole of nature, made like unto God and sharing in his divinity. The other is that in the state of corruption and sin he has fallen from that first state and has become like the beasts. These two propositions are equally firm and certain.

Scripture openly declares this when it says in certain places: *My delights were with the sons of men – I will pour out my spirit upon all flesh – Ye are gods*, while saying in others: *All flesh is grass – Man is like the beasts that perish – I said in my heart concerning the estate of the sons of men.*

Whence it is clearly evident that man through grace is made like unto God and shares his divinity, and without grace he is treated like the beasts of the field.

136 *Diversion.* Sometimes, when I set to thinking about the various activities of men, the dangers and troubles which they face at Court, or in war, giving rise to so many quarrels and passions, daring and

often wicked enterprises and so on, I have often said that the sole cause of man's unhappiness is that he does not know how to stay quietly in his room. A man wealthy enough for life's needs would never leave home to go to sea or besiege some fortress if he knew how to stay at home and enjoy it. Men would never spend so much on a commission in the army if they could bear living in town all their lives, and they only seek after the company and diversion of gambling because they do not enjoy staying at home.

But after closer thought, looking for the particular reasons for all our unhappiness now that I knew its general cause, I found one very cogent reason in the natural unhappiness of our feeble mortal condition, so wretched that nothing can console us when we really think about it.

Imagine any situation you like, add up all the blessings with which you could be endowed, to be king is still the finest thing in the world; yet if you imagine one with all the advantages of his rank, but no means of diversion, left to ponder and reflect on what he is, this limp felicity will not keep him going; he is bound to start thinking of all the threats facing him, of possible revolts, finally of inescapable death and disease, with the result that if he is deprived of so-called diversion he is unhappy, indeed more unhappy than the humblest of his subjects who can enjoy sport and diversion.

The only good thing for men therefore is to be diverted from thinking of what they are, either by some occupation which takes their mind off it, or by some novel and agreeable passion which keeps them busy, like gambling, hunting, some absorbing show, in short by what is called diversion.

That is why gaming and feminine society, war and high office are so popular. It is not that they really bring happiness, nor that anyone imagines that true bliss comes from possessing the money to be won at gaming or the hare that is hunted: no one would take it as a gift. What people want is not the easy peaceful life that allows us to think of our unhappy condition, nor the dangers of war, nor the burdens of office, but the agitation that takes our mind off it and diverts us. That is why we prefer the hunt to the capture.

That is why men are so fond of hustle and bustle; that is why prison is such a fearful punishment; that is why the pleasures of solitude are so incomprehensible. That, in fact, is the main joy of being a king, because people are continually trying to divert him and procure him every kind of pleasure. A king is surrounded by people whose only thought is to divert him and stop him thinking about himself, because, king though he is, he becomes unhappy as soon as he thinks about himself.

That is all that men have been able to devise for attaining happiness; those who philosophize about it, holding that people are quite unreasonable to spend all day chasing a hare that they would not have wanted to buy, have little knowledge of our nature. The hare itself would not save us from thinking about death and the miseries distracting us, but hunting it does so. Thus when Pyrrhus was advised to take the rest towards which he was so strenuously striving, he found it very hard to do so.*

Telling a man to rest is the same as telling him to live happily. It means advising him to enjoy a completely happy state in which he can contemplate at leisure without cause for distress. It means not understanding nature.

Thus men who are naturally conscious of what they are shun nothing so much as rest; they would do anything to be disturbed.

It is wrong then to blame them; they are not wrong to want excitement – if they only wanted it for the sake of diversion. The trouble is that they want it as though, once they had the things they seek, they could not fail to be truly happy. That is what justifies calling their search a vain one. All this shows that neither the critics nor the criticized understand man's real nature.

When men are reproached for pursuing so eagerly something that could never satisfy them, their proper answer, if they really thought about it, ought to be that they simply want a violent and vigorous occupation to take their minds off themselves, and that is why they choose some attractive object to entice them in ardent pursuit. Their opponents could find no answer to that,

---

* [Pyrrhus, pressed to justify his plans for world conquest, reputedly answered that his ultimate purpose was to rest content, but not before realizing his dreams of conquest.]

(Vanity, pleasure of showing off. Dancing, you must think where to put your feet.)

but they do not answer like that because they do not know themselves. They do not know that all they want is the hunt and not the capture. The nobleman sincerely believes that hunting is a great sport, the sport of kings, but his huntsman does not feel like that. They imagine that if they secured a certain appointment they would enjoy resting afterwards, and they do not realize the insatiable nature of cupidity. They think they genuinely want rest when all they really want is activity.

They have a secret instinct driving them to seek external diversion and occupation, and this is the result of their constant sense of wretchedness. They have another secret instinct, left over from the greatness of our original nature, telling them that the only true happiness lies in rest and not in excitement. These two contrary instincts give rise to a confused plan buried out of sight in the depths of their soul, which leads them to seek rest by way of activity and always to imagine that the satisfaction they miss will come to them once they overcome certain obvious difficulties and can open the door to welcome rest.

All our life passes in this way: we seek rest by struggling against certain obstacles, and once they are overcome, rest proves intolerable because of the boredom it produces. We must get away from it and crave excitement.

We think either of present or of threatened

miseries, and even if we felt quite safe on every side, boredom on its own account would not fail to emerge from the depths of our hearts, where it is naturally rooted, and poison our whole mind.

Man is so unhappy that he would be bored even if he had no cause for boredom, by the very nature of his temperament, and he is so vain that, though he has a thousand and one basic reasons for being bored, the slightest thing, like pushing a ball with a billiard cue, will be enough to divert him.

'But,' you will say, 'what is his object in all this?' Just so that he can boast tomorrow to his friends that he played better than someone else. Likewise others sweat away in their studies to prove to scholars that they have solved some hitherto insoluble problem in algebra. Many others again, just as foolishly in my view, risk the greatest dangers so that they can boast afterwards of having captured some stronghold. Then there are others who exhaust themselves observing all these things, not in order to become wiser, but just to show they know them, and these are the biggest fools of the lot, because they know what they are doing, while it is conceivable that the rest would stop being foolish if they knew too.

A given man lives a life free from boredom by gambling a small sum every day. Give him every morning the money he might win that day, but on condition that he does not gamble, and you will make him unhappy. It might be argued that what he wants is the entertainment of gaming and not the winnings. Make him play then for nothing; his interest will not be fired and he will become bored, so it is not just entertainment he wants. A half-hearted entertainment without excitement will bore him. He must have excitement, he must delude himself into imagining that he would be happy to win what he would not want as a gift if it meant giving up gambling. He must create some target for his passions and then arouse his desire, anger, fear, for this object he has created, just like children taking fright at a face they have daubed themselves.

That is why this man, who lost his only son a few months ago and was so troubled and oppressed this morning by lawsuits and quarrels, is not thinking about it any more. Do not be surprised; he is concentrating all his attention on which way the boar will go that his dogs have been so hotly pursuing for the past six hours. That is all he needs. However sad a man may be, if you can persuade him to take up some diversion he will be happy while it lasts, and however happy a man may be, if he lacks diversion and has no absorbing passion or entertainment to keep boredom away, he will soon be depressed and unhappy. Without diversion there is no joy; with diversion there is no sadness. That is what constitutes the happiness of persons of rank, for they have a number of people to divert them and the ability to keep themselves in this state.

Make no mistake about it. What else does it mean to be Superintendent, Chancellor, Chief Justice, but to enjoy a position in which a great number of people come every morning from all parts and do not leave them a single hour of the day to think about themselves? When they are in disgrace and sent off to their country houses, where they lack neither wealth nor servants to meet their needs, they infallibly become miserable and dejected because no one stops them thinking about themselves.

139 *Diversion.* From childhood on men are made responsible for the care of their honour, their property, their friends, and even of the property and honour of their friends; they are burdened with duties, language-training and exercises, and given to understand that they can never be happy unless their health, their honour, their fortune and those of their friends are in good shape, and that it needs only one thing to go wrong to make them unhappy. So they are given responsibilities and duties which harass them from the first moment of each day. You will say that is an odd way to make them happy: what better means could one devise to make them unhappy? What could one do? You would only have to take away all their cares, and then they would see themselves and think about what they are, where they come from, and where they are going. That is why men cannot be too much occupied and distracted, and that is why, when they have been given so many things to do, if they have some time off they are advised to spend it on diversion and sport, and always to keep themselves fully occupied.

How hollow and foul is the heart of man!

148 Man without faith can know neither true good nor justice.

All men seek happiness. There are no exceptions. However different the means they may employ, they all strive towards this goal. The reason why some go to war and some do not is the same desire in both, but interpreted in two different ways. The will never takes the least step except to that end. This is the motive of every act of every man, including those who go and hang themselves.

Yet for very many years no one without faith has ever reached the goal at which everyone is continually aiming. All men complain: princes, subjects, nobles, commoners, old, young, strong, weak, learned, ignorant, healthy, sick, in every country, at every time, of all ages, and all conditions.

A test which has gone on so long, without pause or change, really ought to convince us that we are incapable of attaining the good by our own efforts. But example teaches us very little. No two examples are so exactly alike that there is not some subtle difference, and that is what makes us expect that our expectations will not be disappointed this time as they were last time. So, while the present never satisfies us, experience deceives us, and leads us on from one misfortune to another until death comes as the ultimate and eternal climax.

What else does this craving, and this helplessness, proclaim but that there was once in man a true happiness, of which all that now remains is the empty print and trace? This he tries in vain to fill with everything around him, seeking in things that are not there the help he cannot find in those that are, though none can help, since this infinite abyss can be filled only with an infinite and immutable object; in other words by God himself.

God alone is man's true good, and since man abandoned him it is a strange fact that nothing in nature has been found to take his place: stars, sky, earth, elements, plants, cabbages, leeks, animals, insects, calves, serpents, fever, plague, war, famine, vice, adultery, incest. Since losing his true good, man is capable of seeing it in anything, even his own destruction, although it is so contrary at once to God, to reason and to nature.

Some seek their good in authority, some in intellectual inquiry and knowledge, some in pleasure.

Others again, who have indeed come closer to it, have found it impossible that this universal good, desired by all men, should lie in any of the particular objects which can only be possessed by one individual and which, once shared, cause their possessors more grief over the part they lack than satisfaction over the part they enjoy as their own. They have realized that the true good must be such that it may be possessed by all men at once without diminution or envy, and that no one should be able to lose it against his will. Their reason is that this desire is natural to man, since all men inevitably feel it, and man cannot be without it, and they therefore conclude . . .

151 It is absurd of us to rely on the company of our fellows, as wretched and helpless as we are; they will not help us; we shall die alone.

  We must act then as if we were alone. If that were so, would we build superb houses, etc.? We should unhesitatingly look for the truth. And, if we refuse, it shows that we have a higher regard for men's esteem than for pursuing the truth.

152 Between us and heaven or hell there is only life half-way, the most fragile thing in the world.

153 What after all do you promise me but ten years of self-love (for ten years is the stake), trying hard to please without succeeding, not to speak of certain anguish?

155 Heart
   Instinct
   Principles.

156 Pity the atheists who seek, for are they not unhappy enough? Inveigh against those who boast about it.

157 Atheism indicates strength of mind, but only up to a certain point.

158 As far as the choices go, you must take the trouble to seek the truth, for if you die without worshipping the true principle you are lost. 'But', you say, 'if he had wanted me to worship him, he would have left me some signs of his will.' So he did, but you pay no heed. Look for them then; it is well worth it.

159 If we ought to give up one week of our life, we
ought to give up a hundred years.

160 There are only three sorts of people: those who
have found God and serve him; those who are busy
seeking him and have not found him; those who
live without either seeking or finding him. The first
are reasonable and happy, the last are foolish and
unhappy, those in the middle are unhappy and
reasonable.

161 Atheists should say things that are perfectly clear.
Now it is not perfectly clear that the soul is material.

162 Begin by pitying unbelievers; their condition makes
them unhappy enough.

They ought not to be abused unless it does them
good, but in fact it does them harm.

163 A man in a dungeon, not knowing whether sentence
has been passed on him, with only an hour left to find
out, and that hour enough, once he knows it has been
passed, to have it revoked. It would be unnatural
for him to spend that hour not finding out whether
sentence has been passed but playing piquet.

So it is beyond all nature that man, etc. . . . It is
weighing down the hand of God.

So it is not only the zeal of those who seek him
that proves God's existence, but also the blindness
of those who do not seek him.

164 *Beginning. Dungeon.* I agree that Copernicus' opinion
need not be more closely examined. But this:

It affects our whole life to know whether the soul is mortal or immortal.

165 The last act is bloody, however fine the rest of the play. They throw earth over your head and it is finished for ever.

166 We run heedlessly into the abyss after putting something in front of us to stop us seeing it.

193 *Prejudice leading to error.* It is deplorable to see everybody debating about the means, never the end. Everyone thinks about how he will get on in his career, but when it comes to choosing a career or a country it is fate that decides for us.

It is pitiful to see so many Turks, heretics, unbelievers follow in their fathers' footsteps, solely because they have all been brought up to believe that this is the best course. This is what makes each of us pick his particular career as locksmith, soldier, etc.

That is why savages do not care about Provence.

194 Why have limits been set upon my knowledge, my height, my life, making it a hundred rather than a thousand years? For what reason did nature make it so, and choose this rather than that mean from the whole of infinity, when there is no more reason to choose one rather than another, as none is more attractive than another?

195 *Little of everything.* As we cannot be universal by knowing everything there is to be known about

43

everything, we must know a little about everything, because it is much better to know something about everything than everything about something. Such universality is the finest. It would be still better if we could have both together, but, if a choice must be made, this is the one to choose. The world knows this and does so, for the world is often a good judge.

196 Some fancy makes me dislike people who croak or who puff while eating. Fancy carries a lot of weight. What good will that do us? That we indulge it because it is natural? No, rather that we resist it.

197 There is no better proof of human vanity than to consider the causes and effects of love, because the whole universe can be changed by it. Cleopatra's nose.

198 When I see the blind and wretched state of man, when I survey the whole universe in its dumbness and man left to himself with no light, as though lost in this corner of the universe, without knowing who put him there, what he has come to do, what will become of him when he dies, incapable of knowing anything, I am moved to terror, like a man transported in his sleep to some terrifying desert island, who wakes up quite lost and with no means of escape. Then I marvel that so wretched a state does not drive people to despair. I see other people around me, made like myself. I ask them if they are any better informed than I, and they say they are not. Then these lost and wretched creatures look

around and find some attractive objects to which they become addicted and attached. For my part I have never been able to form such attachments, and considering how very likely it is that there exists something besides what I can see, I have tried to find out whether God has left any traces of himself.

I see a number of religions in conflict, and therefore all false, except one. Each of them wishes to be believed on its own authority and threatens unbelievers. I do not believe them on that account. Anyone can say that. Anyone can call himself a prophet, but I see Christianity, and find its prophecies, which are not something that anyone can do.

199 *Disproportion of man.* This is where unaided knowledge brings us. If it is not true, there is no truth in man, and if it is true, he has good cause to feel humiliated; in either case he is obliged to humble himself.

And, since he cannot exist without believing this knowledge, before going on to a wider inquiry concerning nature, I want him to consider nature just once, seriously and at leisure, and to look at himself as well, and judge whether there is any proportion between himself and nature by comparing the two.

Let man then contemplate the whole of nature in her full and lofty majesty, let him turn his gaze away from the lowly objects around him; let him behold the dazzling light set like an eternal lamp to light up the universe, let him see the earth as a mere speck compared to the vast orbit described by this star, and let him marvel at finding this vast orbit itself to be no more than the tiniest point compared to that described by the stars revolving in the firmament. But if our eyes stop there, let our imagination proceed further; it will grow weary of conceiving things before nature tires of producing them. The whole visible world is only an imperceptible dot in nature's ample bosom. No idea comes near it; it is no good inflating our conceptions beyond imaginable space, we only bring forth atoms compared to the reality of things. Nature is an infinite sphere whose centre is everywhere and circumference nowhere. In short it is the greatest perceptible mark of God's omnipotence that our imagination should lose itself in that thought.

Let man, returning to himself, consider what he is in comparison with what exists; let him regard himself as lost, and from this little dungeon, in which he finds himself lodged, I mean the universe, let him learn to take the earth, its realms, its cities, its houses and himself at their proper value.

What is a man in the infinite?

But, to offer him another prodigy equally astounding, let him look into the tiniest things he knows. Let a mite show him in its minute body incomparably more minute parts, legs with joints, veins in its legs, blood in the veins, humours in the blood, drops in the humours, vapours in the drops: let him divide these things still further until he has exhausted his powers of imagination, and let the last thing he comes down to now be the subject of our discourse. He will perhaps think that this is the ultimate of minuteness in nature.

I want to show him a new abyss. I want to depict to him not only the visible universe, but all the conceivable immensity of nature enclosed in this miniature atom. Let him see there an infinity of universes, each with its firmament, its planets, its earth, in the same proportions as in the visible world, and on that earth animals, and finally mites, in which he will find again the same results as in the first; and finding the same thing yet again in the others without end or respite, he will be lost in such wonders, as astounding in their minuteness as the others in their amplitude. For who will not marvel that our body, a moment ago imperceptible in a universe, itself imperceptible in the bosom of the whole, should now be a colossus, a world, or rather a whole, compared to the nothingness beyond our reach? Anyone who considers himself in this way will be terrified at himself, and, seeing his mass, as given him by nature, supporting him between these two abysses of infinity and nothingness, will tremble at these marvels. I believe that with his curiosity changing into wonder he will be more disposed to contemplate them in silence than investigate them with presumption.

For, after all, what is man in nature? A nothing compared to the infinite, a whole compared to the nothing, a middle point between all and nothing, infinitely remote from an understanding of the extremes; the end of things and their principles are unattainably hidden from him in impenetrable secrecy.

Equally incapable of seeing the nothingness from which he emerges and the infinity in which he is engulfed.

What else can he do, then, but perceive some semblance of the middle of things, eternally hopeless of knowing either their principles or their end? All things have come out of nothingness and are carried onwards to infinity. Who can follow these astonishing processes? The author of these wonders understands them: no one else can.

Because they failed to contemplate these infinities, men have rashly undertaken to probe into nature as if there were some proportion between themselves and her.

Strangely enough they wanted to know the principles of things and go on from there to know everything, inspired by a presumption as infinite as their object. For there can be no doubt that such a plan could not be conceived without infinite presumption or a capacity as infinite as that of nature.

When we know better, we understand that, since nature has engraved her own image and that of her author on all things, they almost all share her double infinity. Thus we see that all the sciences are infinite in the range of their researches, for who can doubt that mathematics, for instance, has an infinity of infinities of propositions to expound? They are infinite also in the multiplicity and subtlety of their principles, for anyone can see that those which are supposed to be ultimate do not stand by themselves, but depend on others, which depend on others again, and thus never allow of any finality.

But we treat as ultimate those which seem so to our reason, as in material things we call a point indivisible when our senses can perceive nothing beyond it, although by its nature it is infinitely divisible.

Of these two infinites of science, that of greatness is much more obvious, and that is why it has occurred to few people to claim that they know everything. 'I am going to speak about everything,' Democritus used to say.

But the infinitely small is much harder to see. The philosophers have much more readily claimed to have reached it, and that is where they have all tripped up. This is the origin of such familiar titles as *Of the principles of things*, *Of the principles of philosophy*, and the like, which are really as pretentious, though they do not look it, as this blatant one: *Of all that can be known*.

We naturally believe we are more capable of reaching the centre of things than of embracing their circumference, and the visible extent of the world is visibly greater than we. But since we in our turn are greater than small things, we think we are more capable of mastering them, and yet it takes no less capacity to reach nothingness than the whole. In either case it takes an infinite capacity, and it seems to me that anyone who had understood the ultimate principles of things might also succeed in knowing infinity. One depends on the other, and one leads to the other. These extremes touch and join by going in opposite directions, and they meet in God and God alone.

Let us then realize our limitations. We are something and we are not everything. Such being as we have conceals from us the knowledge of first principles, which arise from nothingness, and the smallness of our being hides infinity from our sight.

Our intelligence occupies the same rank in the order of intellect as our body in the whole range of nature.

Limited in every respect, we find this intermediate state between two extremes reflected in all our faculties. Our senses can perceive nothing extreme; too much noise deafens us, too much light dazzles; when we are too far or too close we cannot see properly; an argument is obscured by being too long or too short; too much truth bewilders us. I know people who cannot understand that 4 from 0 leaves 0. First principles are too obvious for us; too much pleasure causes discomfort; too much harmony in music is displeasing; too much kindness annoys us: we want to be able to pay back the debt with something over. *Kindness is welcome to the extent that it seems the debt can be paid back. When it goes too far gratitude turns into hatred.*

We feel neither extreme heat nor extreme cold. Qualities carried to excess are bad for us and cannot be perceived; we no longer feel them, we suffer them. Excessive youth and excessive age impair thought; so do too much and too little learning.

In a word, extremes are as if they did not exist for us nor we for them; they escape us or we escape them.

Such is our true state. That is what makes us incapable of certain knowledge or absolute ignorance. We are floating in a medium of vast extent, always drifting uncertainly, blown to and fro; whenever we think we have a fixed point to which we can cling and make fast, it shifts and leaves us behind; if we follow it, it eludes our grasp, slips away, and flees eternally before us. Nothing stands still for us. This is our natural state and yet the state most contrary to our inclinations. We burn with desire to find a firm footing, an ultimate, lasting base on which to build a tower rising up to infinity, but our whole foundation cracks and the earth opens up into the depth of the abyss.

Let us then seek neither assurance nor stability; our reason is always deceived by the inconsistency of appearances; nothing can fix the finite between the two infinites which enclose and evade it.

Once that is clearly understood, I think that each of us can stay quietly in the state in which nature has placed him. Since the middle station allotted to us is always far from the extremes, what does it matter if someone else has a slightly better understanding of things? If he has, and if he takes them a little further, is he not still infinitely remote from the goal? Is not our span of life equally infinitesimal in eternity, even if it is extended by ten years?

In the perspective of these infinites, all finites are equal and I see no reason to settle our imagination on one rather than another. Merely comparing ourselves with the finite is painful.

If man studied himself, he would see how incapable he is of going further. How could a part possibly know the whole? But perhaps he will aspire to know at least the parts to which he bears some proportion. But the parts of the world are all so related and linked together that I think it is impossible to know one without the other and without the whole.

There is, for example, a relationship between man and all he knows. He needs space to contain him, time to exist in, motion to be alive, elements to constitute him, warmth and food for nourishment, air to breathe. He sees light, he feels bodies, everything in short is related to him. To understand man therefore one must know why he needs air to live, and to understand air one must know how it comes to be thus related to the life of man, etc.

Flame cannot exist without air, so, to know one, one must know the other.

Thus, since all things are both caused or causing, assisted and assisting, mediate and immediate, providing mutual support in a chain linking together naturally and imperceptibly the most distant and

us then strive to think well; that is the basic principle of morality.

201 The eternal silence of these infinite spaces fills me with dread.

202 Be comforted; it is not from yourself that you must expect it, but on the contrary you must expect it by expecting nothing from yourself.

271 All Jesus did was to teach men that they loved themselves, that they were slaves, blind, sick, unhappy and sinful, that he had to deliver, enlighten, sanctify and heal them, that this would be achieved by men hating themselves and following him through his misery and death on the Cross.

273 Those who find it hard to believe seek an excuse in the fact that the Jews do not believe. 'If it is so clear,' they say, 'why do they not believe?' They would almost like them to believe so that they should not be deterred by the example of the Jews' refusal. But it is the very fact of their refusal that is the basis of our belief. We should be much less inclined to believe if they were on our side; we should then have a much better excuse.

It is a wonderful thing to have made the Jews so fond of prophecies and so hostile to their fulfilment.

281 *Perpetuity.* This religion consists in believing that man has fallen from a state of glory and communion with God into a state of gloom, penitence and estrangement from God, but that after this life we

shall be restored by a promised Messiah, and it has always existed on earth.

All things have passed away, but this, through which all things are, has endured.

In the first age of the world men were led into all kinds of misdeeds, and yet there were holy men like Enoch, Lamech and others who patiently awaited the Christ promised since the world began. Noah saw men's wickedness at its height, and he had the merit to save the world in his person, through hoping in the Messiah, whom he prefigured. Abraham was surrounded by idolaters when God showed him the mystery of the Messiah whom he hailed from afar. In the time of Isaac and Jacob abomination spread over the whole earth but these holy men lived in their faith, and Jacob on his deathbed, as he was blessing his children, cried out in a rapture which made him interrupt his speech: 'I await the saviour whom thou hast promised, O Lord.'

The Egyptians were riddled with idolatry and magic, and even the people of God were carried away by their example. Yet Moses and others saw him they did not see, and worshipped as they looked to the eternal gifts he was preparing for them.

Next the Greeks and Latins set up false gods. The poets invented a hundred different theologies, the philosophers split up into a thousand different sects. And yet in the heart of Judaea there were always chosen men foretelling the coming of the Messiah who was known only to them. He came at last in the fullness of time, and since then we have seen so many schisms and heresies arise, so many states overthrown, so many changes of every kind, while the Church which worships him who has always been has continued without a break. What is wonderful, incomparable and wholly divine is that this religion which has always survived has always been under attack. Times without number it has been on the verge of total destruction, and every time it has been in such a state God has rescued it by extraordinary manifestations of his power. For what is amazing is that it has continued without bending and bowing to the will of tyrants, for there is nothing strange in a state still surviving when its laws are sometimes made to give way to necessity, but that ... (See the circle in Montaigne.)

284 The only religion which is against nature, against common sense and against our pleasures is the only one which has always existed.

308 The infinite distance between body and mind symbolizes the infinitely more infinite distance between mind and charity, for charity is supernatural.

All the splendour of greatness lacks lustre for those engaged in pursuits of the mind.

The greatness of intellectual people is not visible to kings, rich men, captains, who are all great in a carnal sense.

The greatness of wisdom, which is nothing if it

does not come from God, is not visible to carnal or intellectual people. They are three orders differing in kind.

Great geniuses have their power, their splendour, their greatness, their victory and their lustre, and do not need carnal greatness, which has no relevance for them. They are recognized not with the eyes but with the mind, and that is enough.

Saints have their power, their splendour, their victory, their lustre, and do not need either carnal or intellectual greatness, which has no relevance for them, for it neither adds nor takes away anything. They are recognized by God and the angels, and not by bodies or by curious minds. God is enough for them.

Archimedes in obscurity would still be revered. He fought no battles visible to the eyes, but enriched every mind with his discoveries. How splendidly he shone in the minds of men!

Jesus without wealth or any outward show of knowledge has his own order of holiness. He made no discoveries; he did not reign, but he was humble, patient, thrice holy to God, terrible to devils, and without sin. With what great pomp and marvellously magnificent array he came in the eyes of the heart, which perceive wisdom!

It would have been pointless for Archimedes to play the prince in his mathematical books, prince though he was.

It would have been pointless for Our Lord Jesus Christ to come as a king with splendour in his reign of holiness, but he truly came in splendour in his own order.

It is quite absurd to be shocked at the lowliness of Jesus, as if his lowliness was of the same order as the greatness he came to reveal.

If we consider his greatness in his life, his passion, his obscurity, his death, in the way he chose his disciples, in their desertion, in his secret resurrection and all the rest, we shall see that it is so great that we have no reason to be shocked at a lowliness which has nothing to do with it.

But there are some who are only capable of admiring carnal greatness, as if there were no such thing as greatness of the mind. And others who only admire greatness of the mind, as if there were not infinitely higher greatness in wisdom.

All bodies, the firmament, the stars, the earth and its kingdoms are not worth the least of minds, for it knows them all and itself too, while bodies know nothing.

All bodies together and all minds together and all their products are not worth the least impulse of charity. This is of an infinitely superior order.

Out of all bodies together we could not succeed in creating one little thought. It is impossible, and of a different order. Out of all bodies and minds we could not extract one impulse of true charity. It is impossible, and of a different, supernatural, order.

310 *Proofs of Jesus Christ.* The hypothesis that the Apostles were knaves is quite absurd. Follow it out

to the end and imagine these twelve men meeting after Jesus's death and conspiring to say that he had risen from the dead. This means attacking all the powers that be. The human heart is singularly susceptible to fickleness, to change, to promises, to bribery. One of them had only to deny his story under these inducements, or still more because of possible imprisonment, tortures and death, and they would all have been lost. Follow that out.

332 *Prophecies*. If a single man had written a book fore-telling the time and manner of Jesus's coming and Jesus had come in conformity with these prophecies, this would carry infinite weight.

But there is much more here. There is a succession of men over a period of 4,000 years, coming consistently and invariably one after the other, to foretell the same coming; there is an entire people proclaiming it, existing for 4,000 years to testify in a body to the certainty they feel about it, from which they cannot be deflected by whatever threats and persecutions they may suffer. This is of a quite different order of importance.

335 The most weighty proofs of Jesus are the prophecies. It is for them that God made most provision, for the event which fulfilled them is a miracle, continuing from the birth of the Church to the end. Thus God raised up prophets for 1,600 years and for 400 years afterwards dispersed all the prophecies with all the Jews, who carried them into every corner of the world. Such was the preparation for

the birth of Christ, and, since his Gospel had to be believed by the whole world, there not only had to be prophecies to make men believe it, but these prophecies had to be spread throughout the world so that the whole world should embrace it.

351 Christianity is strange; it bids man to recognize that he is vile, and even abominable, and bids him want to be like God. Without such a counterweight his exaltation would make him horribly vain or his abasement horribly abject.

352 Wretchedness induces despair.

Pride induces presumption.

The Incarnation shows man the greatness of his wretchedness through the greatness of the remedy required.

356 What difference is there between a soldier and a Carthusian as regards obedience? For they are equally obedient and dependent and engaged in equally arduous exercises. But the soldier always hopes to become his own master, and never does, for even captains and princes are always slaves and dependent, but he always hopes, and always strives to achieve his object, whereas the Carthusian vows never to be anything but dependent. Thus they do not differ in their perpetual servitude, which is always their common lot, but in the hope that one always and the other never entertains.

373 We must love God alone and hate ourselves alone.

If the foot had never known it belonged to the

body, and that there was a body on which it depended, if it had only known and loved itself, and if it then came to know that it belonged to a body on which it depended, what regret, what shame it would feel for its past life, for having been useless to the body which poured life into it, and would have annihilated it if it had rejected and cut it off as the foot cut itself off from the body! How it would pray to be kept on! How submissively it would let itself be governed by the will in charge of the body, to the point of being amputated if necessary! Otherwise it would cease to be a member, for every member must be willing to perish for the sake of the body, for whose sake alone everything exists.

378 'If I had seen a miracle,' they say, 'I should be converted.' How can they be positive that they would do what they know nothing about? They imagine that such a conversion consists in a worship of God conducted, as they picture it, like some exchange or conversation. True conversion consists in self-annihilation before the universal being whom we have so often vexed and who is perfectly entitled to destroy us at any moment, in recognizing that we can do nothing without him and that we have deserved nothing but his disfavour. It consists in knowing that there is an irreconcilable opposition between God and us, and that without a mediator there can be no exchange.

392 *Figures.* God wishing to create for himself a holy people, whom he would keep apart from all other

nations, whom he would deliver from their enemies, whom he would bring to a place of rest, promised to do so and foretold by his prophets the time and manner of his coming. And yet to strengthen the hope of his chosen people in every age he showed them an image of all this, never leaving them without assurances of his power and will for their salvation, for in the creation of man Adam was witness to this and received the promise of a saviour who should be born of woman.

When men were still so close to Creation that they had not been able to forget their creation and their fall; when those who had seen Adam were no longer in this world, God sent Noah, saving him and drowning the whole earth by a miracle which clearly showed his power to save the world, and his will to do so, and to cause to be born from the seed of woman the one he had promised.

This miracle was sufficient to strengthen the hope of the elect.

The memory of the Flood being still so fresh among men, while Noah was still alive, God made his promises to Abraham, and while Shem was still alive, God sent Moses . . .

403 *Wretchedness*. Solomon and Job have known and spoken best about man's wretchedness, one the happiest, the other the unhappiest of men; one knowing by experience the vanity of pleasure, and the other the reality of afflictions.

412 Men are so inevitably mad that not to be mad would
be to give a mad twist to madness.

414 *Wretchedness.* The only thing that consoles us for
our miseries is diversion. And yet it is the greatest
of our miseries. For it is that above all which pre-
vents us thinking about ourselves and leads us
imperceptibly to destruction. But for that we should
be bored, and boredom would drive us to seek
some more solid means of escape, but diversion
passes our time and brings us imperceptibly to our
death.

418 *Infinity – nothing.* [THE WAGER] Our soul is cast into
the body where it finds number, time, dimensions;
it reasons about these things and calls them natural,
or necessary, and can believe nothing else.

Unity added to infinity does not increase it at all,
any more than a foot added to an infinite measure-
ment: the finite is annihilated in the presence of the
infinite and becomes pure nothingness. So it is with
our mind before God, with our justice before divine
justice. There is not so great a disproportion between our justice and God's as between unity and
infinity.

God's justice must be as vast as his mercy. Now
his justice towards the damned is less vast and ought
to be less startling to us than his mercy towards the
elect.

We know that the infinite exists without knowing
its nature, just as we know that it is untrue that
numbers are finite. Thus it is true that there is an

infinite number, but we do not know what it is. It is untrue that it is even, untrue that it is odd, for by adding a unit it does not change its nature. Yet it is a number, and every number is even or odd. (It is true that this applies to every finite number.)

Therefore we may well know that God exists without knowing what he is.

Is there no substantial truth, seeing that there are so many true things which are not truth itself?

Thus we know the existence and nature of the finite because we too are finite and extended in space.

We know the existence of the infinite without knowing its nature, because it too has extension but unlike us no limits.

But we do not know either the existence or the nature of God, because he has neither extension nor limits.

But by faith we know his existence, through glory we shall know his nature.

Now I have already proved that it is quite possible to know that something exists without knowing its nature.

Let us now speak according to our natural lights.

If there is a God, he is infinitely beyond our comprehension, since, being indivisible and without limits, he bears no relation to us. We are therefore incapable of knowing either what he is or whether he is. That being so, who would dare to attempt an answer to the question? Certainly not we, who bear no relation to him.

Who then will condemn Christians for being unable to give rational grounds for their belief, professing as they do a religion for which they cannot give rational grounds? They declare that it is a folly, *stultitiam*, in expounding it to the world, and then you complain that they do not prove it. If they did prove it they would not be keeping their word. It is by being without proof that they show they are not without sense. 'Yes, but although that excuses those who offer their religion as such, and absolves them from the criticism of producing it without rational grounds, it does not absolve those who accept it.' Let us then examine this point, and let us say: 'Either God is or he is not.' But to which view shall we be inclined? Reason cannot decide this question. Infinite chaos separates us. At the far end of this infinite distance a coin is being spun which will come down heads or tails. How will you wager? Reason cannot make you choose either, reason cannot prove either wrong.

Do not then condemn as wrong those who have made a choice, for you know nothing about it. 'No, but I will condemn them not for having made this particular choice, but any choice, for, although the one who calls heads and the other one are equally at fault, the fact is that they are both at fault: the right thing is not to wager at all.'

Yes, but you must wager. There is no choice, you are already committed. Which will you choose then? Let us see: since a choice must be made, let us see which offers you the least interest. You have two things to lose: the true and the good; and two things to stake: your reason and your will, your knowledge and your happiness; and your nature has two things to avoid: error and wretchedness. Since you must necessarily choose, your reason is no more affronted by choosing one rather than the other. That is one point cleared up. But your happiness? Let us weigh up the gain and the loss involved in calling heads that God exists. Let us assess the two cases: if you win you win everything, if you lose you lose nothing. Do not hesitate then; wager that he does exist. 'That is wonderful. Yes, I must wager, but perhaps I am wagering too much.' Let us see: since there is an equal chance of gain and loss, if you stood to win only two lives for one you could still wager, but supposing you stood to win three?

You would have to play (since you must necessarily play) and it would be unwise of you, once you are obliged to play, not to risk your life in order to win three lives at a game in which there is an equal chance of losing and winning. But there is an eternity of life and happiness. That being so, even though there were an infinite number of chances, of which only one were in your favour, you would still be right to wager one in order to win two; and you would be acting wrongly, being obliged to play, in refusing to stake one life against three in a game, where out of an infinite number of chances there is one in your favour, if there were an infinity of infinitely happy life to be won. But here there is an infinity of infinitely happy life to be won, one chance of winning against a finite number of chances of losing, and what you are staking is finite. That leaves no choice; wherever there is infinity, and where there are not infinite chances of losing against that of winning, there is no room for hesitation, you must give everything. And thus, since you are obliged to play, you must be renouncing reason if you hoard your life rather than risk it for an infinite gain, just as likely to occur as a loss amounting to nothing.

For it is no good saying that it is uncertain whether you will win, that it is certain that you are taking a risk, and that the infinite distance between the certainty of what you are risking and the uncertainty of what you may gain makes the finite good you are certainly risking equal to the infinite good that you are not certain to gain. This is not the case. Every gambler takes a certain risk for an uncertain gain, and yet he is taking a certain finite risk for an uncertain finite gain without sinning against reason. Here there is no infinite distance between the certain risk and the uncertain gain: that is not true. There is, indeed, an infinite distance between the certainty of winning and the certainty of losing, but the proportion between the uncertainty of winning and the certainty of what is being risked is in proportion to the chances of winning or losing. And hence if there are as many chances on one side as on the other you are playing for even odds. And in that case the certainty of what you are risking is equal to the uncertainty of what you may win; it is by no means infinitely distant from it. Thus our argument carries infinite weight, when the stakes are finite in a game where there are even chances of winning and losing and an infinite prize to be won.

This is conclusive and if men are capable of any truth this is it.

'I confess, I admit it, but is there really no way of seeing what the cards are?' – 'Yes. Scripture and the rest, etc.' – 'Yes, but my hands are tied and my lips are sealed; I am being forced to wager and I am not free; I am being held fast and I am so made that I cannot believe. What do you want me to do then?' – 'That is true, but at least get it into your head that, if you are unable to believe, it is because of your passions, since reason impels you to believe and yet you cannot do so. Concentrate then not on convincing yourself by multiplying proofs of God's existence but by diminishing your passions. You want to find faith and you do not know the road. You want to be cured of unbelief and you ask for the remedy: learn from those who were once bound like you and who now wager all they have. These are people who know the road you wish to follow, who have been cured of the affliction of which you wish to be cured: follow the way by which they began. They behaved just as if they did believe, taking holy water, having masses said, and so on. That will make you believe quite naturally, and will make you more docile.' – 'But that is what I am afraid of.' – 'But why? What have you to lose? But to show you that this is the way, the fact is that this diminishes the passions which are your great obstacles . . .'

'Now what harm will come to you from choosing this course? You will be faithful, honest, humble, grateful, full of good works, a sincere, true friend . . . It is true you will not enjoy noxious pleasures, glory and good living, but will you not have others?

'I tell you that you will gain even in this life, and that at every step you take along this road you will see that your gain is so certain and your risk so negligible that in the end you will realize that you have wagered on something certain and infinite for which you have paid nothing.'

'How these words fill me with rapture and delight! –'

'If my words please you and seem cogent, you must know that they come from a man who went down upon his knees before and after to pray this infinite and indivisible being, to whom he submits his own, that he might bring your being also to submit to him for your own good and for his glory: and that strength might thus be reconciled with lowliness.'

427 [AGAINST INDIFFERENCE] Let them at least learn what this religion is which they are attacking before attacking it. If this religion boasted that it had a clear sight of God and plain and manifest evidence

of his existence, it would be an effective objection to say that there is nothing to be seen in the world which proves him so obviously. But since on the contrary it says that men are in darkness and remote from God, that he has hidden himself from their understanding, that this is the very name which he gives himself in Scripture: *Deus absconditus* [the hidden God]; and, in a word, if it strives equally to establish these two facts: that God has appointed visible signs in the Church so that he shall be recognized by those who genuinely seek him, and that he has none the less hidden them in such a way that he will only be perceived by those who seek him with all their heart, then what advantage can they derive when, unconcerned to seek the truth as they profess to be, they protest that nothing shows it to them? For the obscurity in which they find themselves, and which they use as an objection against the Church, simply establishes one of the things the Church maintains without affecting the other, and far from proving her teaching false, confirms it.

In order really to attack the truth they would have to protest that they had made every effort to seek it everywhere, even in what the Church offers by way of instruction, but without any satisfaction. If they talked like that they would indeed be attacking one of Christianity's claims. But I hope to show here that no reasonable person could talk like that. I even venture to say that no one has ever done so. We know well enough how people in this frame of mind behave. They think they have made great efforts to learn when they have spent a few hours reading some book of the Bible, and have questioned some ecclesiastic about the truths of the faith. After that they boast that they have sought without success in books and among men. But, in fact, I should say to them what I have often said: such negligence is intolerable. It is not a question here of the trifling interest of some stranger prompting such behaviour: it is a question of ourselves, and our all.

The immortality of the soul is something of such vital importance to us, affecting us so deeply, that one must have lost all feeling not to care about knowing the facts of the matter. All our actions and thoughts must follow such different paths, according to whether there is hope of eternal blessings or not, that the only possible way of acting with sense and judgement is to decide our course in the light of this point, which ought to be our ultimate objective.

Thus our chief interest and chief duty is to seek enlightenment on this subject, on which all our conduct depends. And that is why, amongst those who are not convinced, I make an absolute distinction between those who strive with all their might to learn and those who live without troubling themselves or thinking about it.

I can feel nothing but compassion for those who sincerely lament their doubt, who regard it as the ultimate misfortune, and who, sparing no effort to escape from it, make their search their principal and most serious business.

But as for those who spend their lives without a thought for this final end of life and who, solely because they do not find within themselves the light of conviction, neglect to look elsewhere, and to examine thoroughly whether this opinion is one of those which people accept out of credulous simplicity or one of those which, though obscure in themselves, none the less have a most solid and unshakeable foundation: as for them, I view them very differently.

This negligence in a matter where they themselves, their eternity, their all are at stake, fills me more with irritation than pity; it astounds and appals me; it seems quite monstrous to me. I do not say this prompted by the pious zeal of spiritual devotion. I mean on the contrary that we ought to have this feeling from principles of human interest and self-esteem. For that we need only see what the least enlightened see.

One needs no great sublimity of soul to realize that in this life there is no true and solid satisfaction, that all our pleasures are mere vanity, that our afflictions are infinite, and finally that death which threatens us at every moment must in a few years infallibly face us with the inescapable and appalling alternative of being annihilated or wretched throughout eternity.

Nothing could be more real, or more dreadful than that. Let us put on as bold a face as we like:

that is the end awaiting the world's most illustrious life. Let us ponder these things, and then say whether it is not beyond doubt that the only good thing in this life is the hope of another life, that we become happy only as we come nearer to it, and that, just as no more unhappiness awaits those who have been quite certain of eternity, so there is no happiness for those who have no inkling of it.

It is therefore quite certainly a great evil to have such doubts, but it is at least an indispensable obligation to seek when one does thus doubt; so the doubter who does not seek is at the same time very unhappy and very wrong. If in addition he feels a calm satisfaction, which he openly professes, and even regards as a reason for joy and vanity, I can find no terms to describe so extravagant a creature.

What can give rise to such feelings? What reason for joy can be found in the expectation of nothing but helpless wretchedness? What reason for vanity in being plunged into impenetrable darkness? And how can such an argument as this occur to a reasonable man?

'I do not know who put me into the world, nor what the world is, nor what I am myself. I am terribly ignorant about everything. I do not know what my body is, or my senses, or my soul, or even that part of me which thinks what I am saying, which reflects about everything and about itself, and does not know itself any better than it knows anything else.

'I see the terrifying spaces of the universe hemming me in, and I find myself attached to one corner of this vast expanse without knowing why I have been put in this place rather than that, or why the brief span of life allotted to me should be assigned to one moment rather than another of all the eternity which went before me and all that which will come after me. I see only infinity on every side, hemming me in like an atom or like the shadow of a fleeting instant. All I know is that I must soon die, but what I know least about is this very death which I cannot evade.

'Just as I do not know whence I come, so I do not know whither I am going. All I know is that when I leave this world I shall fall for ever into nothingness or into the hands of a wrathful God, but I do not know which of these two states is to be my eternal lot. Such is my state, full of weakness and uncertainty. And my conclusion from all this is that I must pass my days without a thought of seeking what is to happen to me. Perhaps I might find some enlightenment in my doubts, but I do not want to take the trouble, nor take a step to look for it: and afterwards, as I sneer at those who are striving to this end – (whatever certainty they have should arouse despair rather than vanity) – I will go without fear or foresight to face so momentous an event, and allow myself to be carried off limply to my death, uncertain of my future state for all eternity.'

Who would wish to have as his friend a man who argued like that? Who would choose him from among others as a confidant in his affairs? Who would resort to him in adversity? To what use in life could he possibly be turned?

It is truly glorious for religion to have such unreasonable men as enemies: their opposition represents so small a danger that it serves on the contrary to establish the truths of religion. For the Christian faith consists almost wholly in establishing these two things: The corruption of nature and the redemption of Christ. Now, I maintain that, if they do not serve to prove the truth of the redemption by the sanctity of their conduct, they do at least admirably serve to prove the corruption of nature by such unnatural sentiments.

Nothing is so important to man as his state: nothing more fearful than eternity. Thus the fact that there exist men who are indifferent to the loss of their being and the peril of an eternity of wretchedness is against nature. With everything else they are quite different; they fear the most trifling things, foresee and feel them; and the same man who spends so many days and nights in fury and despair at losing some office or at some imaginary affront to his honour is the very one who knows that he is going to lose everything through death but feels neither anxiety nor emotion. It is a monstrous thing to see one and the same heart at once so sensitive to minor things and so strangely insensitive to the greatest. It is an incomprehensible spell, a supernatural torpor that points to an omnipotent power as its cause.

Man's nature must have undergone a strange reversal for him to glory in being in a state in which it seems incredible that any single person should be. Yet experience has shown me so many like this that it would be surprising if we did not know that most of those concerned in this are pretending and are not really what they seem. They are people who have heard that it is good form to display such extravagance. This is what they call shaking off the yoke, and what they are trying to imitate. But it would not be difficult to show them how mistaken they are to court esteem in this way. That is not how to acquire it, not even, I would say, among worldly people, who judge things sensibly and who know that the only way to succeed is to appear honest, faithful, judicious and capable of rendering useful service to one's friends, because by nature men only like what may be of use to them. Now what advantage is it to us to hear someone say he has shaken off the yoke, that he does not believe that there is a God watching over his actions, that he considers himself sole master of his behaviour, and that he proposes to account for it to no one but himself? Does he think that by so doing he has henceforth won our full confidence, and made us expect from him consolation, counsel and assistance in all life's needs? Do they think that they have given us great pleasure by telling us that they hold our soul to be no more than wind or smoke, and saying it moreover in tones of pride and satisfaction? Is this then something to be said gaily? Is it not on the contrary something to be said sadly, as being the saddest thing in the world?

If they thought seriously, they would see that this is so misguided, so contrary to good sense, so opposed to decency, so remote in every way from the good form they seek, that they would be more likely to reform than corrupt those who might feel inclined to follow them. And, indeed, make them describe the feeling and reasons which inspire their doubts about religion: what they say will be so feeble and cheap as to persuade you of the contrary. As someone said to them very aptly one day: 'If you go on arguing like that,' he said, 'you really will convert me.' And he was right, for who would not shrink from finding himself sharing the feelings of such contemptible people?

Thus those who only pretend to feel like this would be indeed unhappy if they did violence to their nature in order to become the most impertinent of men. If they are vexed in their inmost heart at not seeing more clearly, they should not try to pretend otherwise: it would be no shame to admit it. There is no shame except in having none. There is no surer sign of extreme weakness of mind than the failure to recognize the unhappy state of a man without God; there is no surer sign of an evil heart than failure to desire that the eternal promises be true; nothing is more cowardly than to brazen it out with God. Let them then leave such impiety to those ill-bred enough to be really capable of it; let them at least be decent people if they cannot be

Christians; let them, in short, acknowledge that there are only two classes of persons who can be called reasonable: those who serve God with all their heart because they know him and those who seek him with all their heart because they do not know him.

As for those who live without either knowing or seeking him, they consider it so little worthwhile to take trouble over themselves that they are not worth other people's trouble, and it takes all the charity of that religion they despise not to despise them to the point of abandoning them to their folly. But as this religion obliges us always to regard them, as long as they live, as being capable of receiving grace which may enlighten them, and to believe that in a short time they may be filled with more faith than we are, while we on the contrary may be stricken by the same blindness which is theirs now, we must do for them what we would wish to be done for us in their place, and appeal to them to have pity on themselves, and to take at least a few steps in an attempt to find some light. Let them spend on reading about it a few of the hours they waste on other things: however reluctantly they may approach the task they will perhaps hit upon something, and at least they will not be losing much. But as for those who approach it with absolute sincerity and a real desire to find the truth, I hope that they will be satisfied, and convinced by the proofs of so divine a religion which I have collected here, following more or less this order . . .

429 This is what I see and what troubles me. I look
around in every direction and all I see is darkness.
Nature has nothing to offer me that does not give
rise to doubt and anxiety. If I saw no sign there of
a Divinity I should decide on a negative solution: if
I saw signs of a Creator everywhere I should peace-
fully settle down in the faith. But, seeing too much
to deny and not enough to affirm, I am in a pitiful
state, where I have wished a hundred times over
that, if there is a God supporting nature, she should
unequivocally proclaim him, and that, if the signs
in nature are deceptive, they should be completely
erased; that nature should say all or nothing so that
I could see what course I ought to follow. Instead
of that, in the state in which I am, not knowing
what I am nor what I ought to do, I know neither
my condition nor my duty. My whole heart strains
to know what the true good is in order to pursue
it: no price would be too high to pay for eternity.

I envy those of the faithful whom I see living so
unconcernedly, making so little use of a gift which,
it seems to me, I should turn to such different
account.

430 No other has realized that man is the most excellent
of creatures. Some, fully realizing how real his excellence is, have taken for cowardice and ingratitude
men's natural feelings of abasement; while others,
fully realizing how real this abasement is, have
treated with haughty ridicule the feelings of greatness which are just as natural to man.

'Lift up your eyes to God,' say some of them, 'look at him whom you resemble and who created you to worship him. You can make yourself like him: wisdom will make you his equal, if you want to follow him.' – 'Hold your heads high, free men,' said Epictetus. And others say, 'Cast down your eyes towards the ground, puny worm that you are, and look at the beasts whose companion you are.'

What then is to become of man? Will he be the equal of God or the beasts? What a terrifying distance! What then shall he be? Who cannot see from all this that man is lost, that he has fallen from his place, that he anxiously seeks it, and cannot find it again? And who then is to direct him there? The greatest men have failed.

434 Imagine a number of men in chains, all under sentence of death, some of whom are each day butchered in the sight of the others; those remaining see their own condition in that of their fellows, and looking at each other with grief and despair await their turn. This is an image of the human condition.

450 The true religion would have to teach greatness and wretchedness, inspire self-esteem and self-contempt, love and hate.

470 The vilest feature of man is the quest for glory, but it is just this that most clearly shows his excellence. For whatever possession he may own on earth, whatever health or essential amenity he may enjoy, he is dissatisfied unless he enjoys the good opinion

of his fellows. He so highly values human reason that, however privileged he may be on earth, if he does not also enjoy a privileged position in human reason he is not happy. This is the finest position on earth, nothing can deflect him from this desire, and this is the most indelible quality in the human heart.

And those who most despise men, and put them on the same level as the beasts, still want to be admired and trusted by them, and contradict themselves by their own feelings, for their nature, which is stronger than anything, convinces them more strongly of man's greatness than reason convinces them of their vileness.

474 When the creation of the world began to recede into the past, God provided a single contemporary historian, and charged an entire people with the custody of this book, so that this should be the most authentic history in the world and all men could learn from it something which it was so necessary for them to know and which could only be known from it.

477 Pride is a counterweight and antidote for all forms of wretchedness. Here is a strange monster, and a very palpable aberration. Here he is, fallen from his place, looking anxiously for it. That is what all men do. Let us see who has found it.

480 In all religions sincerity is essential: true heathens, true Jews, true Christians.

499 What man ever had greater glory?

The entire Jewish people foretells him before his coming. The Gentiles worship him after his coming.

Both the Gentile and Jewish peoples regard him as their centre.

And yet what man ever enjoyed such glory less?

For thirty of his thirty-three years he lives without showing himself. For three years he is treated as an impostor. The priests and rulers reject him. Those who are nearest and dearest to him despise him, finally he dies betrayed by one of his disciples, denied by another and forsaken by all.

What benefit then did he derive from such glory? No man ever had such great glory, no man ever suffered greater ignominy. All this glory has only been of use to us, to enable us to recognize him, and he had none of it for himself.

505 *Authority.* Hearsay is so far from being a criterion of belief that you should not believe anything until you have put yourself into the same state as if you had never heard it.

It is your own inner assent and the consistent voice of your reason rather than that of others which should make you believe.

Belief is so important.

A hundred contradictions might be true.

If antiquity was the criterion of belief, then the ancients had no criterion.

If general consent, if men had died . . . ?

Punishment of sinners: error.

False humility, pride.

Raise the curtain.

You are wasting your time, one must either believe, deny or doubt.

Are we then to have no criterion?

When animals do something we can judge whether they are doing it well; is there to be no criterion for judging men?

Denying, believing and doubting are to men what running is to horses.

510 The more intelligent one is, the more men of originality one finds. Ordinary people find no difference between men.

511 Different kinds of right thinking, some in a particular order of things but not in others where they go quite astray.

Some draw correct conclusions from a small number of principles, and this is one kind of right thinking.

Others draw correct conclusions from things involving numerous principles.

For example, some have a good grasp of the properties of water, which involve few principles, but whose conclusions are so subtle that only an extremely accurate mind can reach them. These people might all the same not be great mathematicians, because mathematics comprises a large number of principles, and a mind may well be such that it can easily get right to the bottom of a few principles without being able to make the least advance in things involving many.

Thus there are two kinds of mind: one goes rapidly and deeply into the conclusions from principles, and this is the accurate mind. The other can grasp a large number of principles and keep them distinct, and this is the mathematical mind. The first is a powerful and precise mind, the second shows breadth of mind. Now it is quite possible to have one without the other, for a mind can be powerful and narrow, as well as broad and weak.

513 *Mathematics. Intuition.* True eloquence has no time for eloquence, true morality has no time for morality. In other words the morality of judgement has no time for the random morality of mind.

For judgement is what goes with instinct, just as knowledge goes with mind. Intuition falls to the lot of judgement, mathematics to that of the mind.

To have no time for philosophy is to be a true philosopher.

517 If St Augustine were to appear today and enjoy as little authority as his modern defenders he would not accomplish anything. God has ruled his Church well by sending him earlier, and endowed with authority.

518 *Scepticism.* – Extreme intelligence is accused of being as foolish as extreme lack of it; only moderation is good. The majority have laid this down and attack anyone who deviates from it towards any extreme whatever. I am not going to be awkward, I readily

consent to being put in the middle and refuse to be at the bottom end, not because it is bottom but because it is the end, for I should refuse just as much to be put at the top. It is deserting humanity to desert the middle way.

The greatness of the human soul lies in knowing how to keep this course; greatness does not mean going outside it, but rather keeping within it.

526 Evil is easy; it has countless forms, while good is almost unique. But a certain sort of evil is as hard to find as what is called good, and this particular evil is often on that account passed off as good. Indeed it takes as much extraordinary greatness of soul to attain such evil, as to attain good.

532 *Scepticism.* I will write down my thoughts here as they come and in a perhaps not aimless confusion. This is the true order and it will always show my aim by its very disorder.

I should be honouring my subject too much if I treated it in order, since I am trying to show that it is incapable of it.

533 We always picture Plato and Aristotle wearing long academic gowns, but they were ordinary decent people like anyone else, who enjoyed a laugh with their friends. And when they amused themselves by composing their *Laws* and *Politics* they did it for fun. It was the least philosophical and least serious part of their lives: the most philosophical part was living simply and without fuss.

If they wrote about politics it was as if to lay down rules for a madhouse.

And if they pretended to treat it as something really important it was because they knew that the madmen they were talking to believed themselves to be kings and emperors. They humoured these beliefs in order to calm down their madness with as little harm as possible.

535 There are some vices which only keep hold on us through other ones, and if we take the trunk away they come off like the branches.

540 All the good maxims already exist in the world: we just fail to apply them.

For example, no one doubts that one should risk his life in defence of the common good, and many people do so, but not for religion.

Inequality must necessarily exist among men, it is true: but that once granted the door is open not only to the most absolute rule but to the most absolute tyranny.

It is necessary to relax the mind a little, but that opens the door to the greatest excesses.

Let us define the limits. There are no boundaries in things. Laws try to impose some, and the mind cannot bear it.

542 Thoughts come at random, and go at random. No device for holding on to them or for having them.

A thought has escaped: I was trying to write it down: instead I write that it has escaped me.

545 'All that is in the world is lust of the flesh, lust of
the eyes or pride of life.' *Libido sentiendi, libido
sciendi, libido dominandi.* Wretched is the cursed land
consumed rather than watered by these three rivers
of fire! Happy are those who are beside those rivers,
neither immersed, nor carried away, but immov-
ably steady beside these rivers, not standing but
sitting, in a low and safe position. They will not rise
thence before the light, but, after resting in peace,
stretch out their hands to him who shall raise them
to stand upright and steady in the porches of Jeru-
salem the blessed, where pride shall no more be
able to fight against them and lay them low; and
yet they weep, not at the sight of all the perishable
things swept away by these torrents, but at the
memory of their beloved home, the heavenly Jeru-
salem, which they constantly remember through
the long years of their exile.

551 Imagination magnifies small objects with fantastic
exaggeration until they fill our soul, and with bold
insolence cuts down great things to its own size, as
when speaking of God.

561 They say that eclipses are portents of disaster,
because disasters are so common, and misfortune
occurs often enough for these forecasts to be right,
whereas if they said that eclipses were portents of
good fortune they would often be wrong. They
ascribe good fortune only to rare conjunctions of
heavenly bodies and thus seldom guess wrong in
their forecasts.

562 There are only two kinds of men: the righteous who think they are sinners and the sinners who think they are righteous.

577 If we must never take any chances we ought not to do anything for religion, for it is not certain. But how many chances we do take: sea voyages, battles. Therefore, I say, we should have to do nothing at all, for nothing is certain. And there is more certainty in religion than that we shall live to see tomorrow.

For it is not certain that we shall see tomorrow but it is certainly possible that we shall not. We cannot say the same of religion. It is not certain that it is true, but who would dare to say that it is certainly possible that it is not?

Now when we work for tomorrow and take chances we are behaving reasonably, for we ought to take chances, according to the rule of probability already demonstrated.

St Augustine saw that we take chances at sea, in battle, etc. – but he did not see the rule of probability which proves that we ought to. Montaigne saw that we are offended by a lame mind and that habit can do anything, but he did not see the reason for this.

All these people saw the effects but did not see the causes. In comparison with those who have discovered the causes they are like those who have only eyes compared to those who have minds. For the effects can, as it were, be felt by the senses but the causes can only be perceived by the mind. And, although these effects can be seen by the mind, this mind can be compared to that which sees the causes as the bodily senses may be compared to the mind.

585 There is a certain model of attractiveness and beauty consisting in a certain relation between our nature, weak or strong as it may be, and the thing which pleases us.

Everything that conforms to this model attracts us, be it a house, a song, a speech, verse, prose, a woman, birds, rivers, trees, rooms, clothes, etc.

Everything which does not conform to this model is displeasing to people of good taste.

And as there is an exact relation between a song and a house based on this good model, because both resemble a single model, though each in its own way, there is in the same way an exact relation between things based on bad models. It is not that there is only one bad model, because they are innumerable, but every bad sonnet, for example, whatever the false model it is based on, is exactly like a woman dressed according to that model.

Nothing gives a better idea of the absurdity of a bad sonnet than to consider its nature and its model and then to imagine a woman or a house conforming to that model.

595 Unless we know ourselves to be full of pride, ambition, concupiscence, weakness, wretchedness and unrighteousness, we are truly blind. And if someone knows all this and does not desire to be saved, what can be said of him?

How then can we have anything but respect for

a religion which knows man's faults so well? What desire but that a religion which promises such desirable remedies should be true?

607 *Figures.* Saviour, father, sacrificer, sacrifice, food, king, wise, lawgiver, afflicted, poor, destined to produce a people whom he should lead and feed, and bring into the land.

620 Man is obviously made for thinking. Therein lies all his dignity and his merit; and his whole duty is to think as he ought. Now the order of thought is to begin with ourselves, and with our author and our end.

Now what does the world think about? Never about that, but about dancing, playing the lute, singing, writing verse, tilting at the ring, etc., and fighting, becoming king, without thinking what it means to be a king or to be a man.

622 *Boredom.* Man finds nothing so intolerable as to be in a state of complete rest, without passions, without occupation, without diversion, without effort.

Then he faces his nullity, loneliness, inadequacy, dependence, helplessness, emptiness.

And at once there wells up from the depths of his soul boredom, gloom, depression, chagrin, resentment, despair.

623 If it is unnatural blindness to live without trying to find out what one is, it is a fearful blindness to lead an evil life while believing in God.

627 Vanity is so firmly anchored in man's heart that a soldier, a camp follower, a cook or a porter will boast and expect admirers, and even philosophers want them; those who write against them want to enjoy the prestige of having written well, those who read them want the prestige of having read them, and perhaps I who write this want the same thing, perhaps my readers . . .

631 It is good to be tired and weary from fruitlessly seeking the true good, so that one can stretch out one's arms to the Redeemer.

632 Man's sensitivity to little things and insensitivity to the greatest things are marks of a strange disorder.

633 Despite the sight of all the miseries which affect us and hold us by the throat we have an irrepressible instinct which bears us up.

634 The most important thing in our lives is the choice of a trade, and chance decides it.

Custom makes masons, soldiers, roofers. 'He is an excellent roofer,' they say, and, speaking of soldiers: 'They are quite mad,' while others on the contrary say: 'There is nothing as great as war, everyone else is worthless.' From hearing people praise these trades in our childhood and running down all the others we make our choice. For we naturally love virtue and hate folly; the very words will decide, we only go wrong in applying them.

So great is the force of custom that where nature

has merely created men, we create every kind and condition of men.

For some regions are full of masons, some of soldiers etc. There is no doubt that nature is not so uniform: it is custom then which does all this, for it coerces nature, but sometimes nature overcomes it and keeps man to his instincts despite all customs, good or bad.

638 When we are well we wonder how we should manage if we were ill. When we are ill we take our medicine cheerfully; our illness settles that problem for us. We no longer have the passions, and the desires for diversions and outings, which went with good health and are incompatible with the exigencies of our illness. Nature then inspires the passions and desires appropriate to our present state. It is only the fears that we owe to ourselves, and not to nature, which disturb us by linking the state in which we are with the passions of that in which we are not.

649 *Montaigne.* What is good in Montaigne can only be acquired with difficulty. What is bad in him, I mean apart from morals, could have been corrected in a moment if someone had warned him that he was making too much of things and talking too much about himself.

668 Each man is everything to himself, for with his death everything is dead for him. That is why each of us thinks he is everything to everyone. We must

not judge nature by ourselves, but by its own standards.

674 We do not keep ourselves virtuous by our own power, but by the counterbalance of two opposing vices, just as we stay upright between two contrary winds. Take one of these vices away and we fall into the other.

685 *Glory.* Animals do not admire each other. A horse does not admire its companion. It is not that they will not race against each other, but this is of no consequence, for, back in the stable, the one who is heavier and clumsier does not on that account give up his oats to the other, as men want others to do to them. With them virtue is its own reward.

688 What is the self?

A man goes to the window to see the people passing by; if I pass by, can I say he went there to see me? No, for he is not thinking of me in particular. But what about a person who loves someone for the sake of her beauty; does he love *her*? No, for smallpox, which will destroy beauty without destroying the person, will put an end to his love for her.

And if someone loves me for my judgement or my memory, do they love me? *me*, myself? No, for I could lose these qualities without losing my self. Where then is this self, if it is neither in the body nor the soul? And how can one love the body or the soul except for the sake of such qualities, which are not what makes up the self, since they are perishable? Would we love the substance of a person's soul, in the abstract, whatever qualities might be in it? That is not possible, and it would be wrong. Therefore we never love anyone, but only qualities.

Let us then stop scoffing at those who win honour through their appointments and offices, for we never love anyone except for borrowed qualities.

693 The easiest conditions to live in from the world's point of view are the hardest from that of God; and vice versa. Nothing is so hard from the world's point of view as the religious life, while nothing is easier from that of God. Nothing is easier than to enjoy high office or great wealth in a worldly way, nothing harder than to live such a life in God's way, without taking interest or pleasure in it.

696 Let no one say that I have said nothing new; the arrangement of the material is new. In playing tennis both players use the same ball, but one plays it better.

I would just as soon be told that I have used old words. As if the same thoughts did not form a different argument by being differently arranged, just as the same words make different thoughts when arranged differently!

697 Those who lead disorderly lives tell those who are normal that it is they who deviate from nature, and think they are following nature themselves; just as

those who are on board ship think that the people on shore are moving away. Language is the same everywhere: we need a fixed point to judge it. The harbour is the judge of those aboard ship, but where are we going to find a harbour in morals?

699 When everything is moving at once, nothing appears to be moving, as on board ship. When everyone is moving towards depravity, no one seems to be moving, but if someone stops he shows up the others who are rushing on, by acting as a fixed point.

709 We know so little about ourselves that many people think they are going to die when they are quite well, and many think they are quite well when they are on the point of death, not sensing the approach of fever or the abscess ready to form.

711 *Strength*. Why do we follow the majority? Is it because they are more right? No, but they are stronger.

Why do we follow ancient laws and opinions? Is it because they are the soundest? No, but they are unique and leave us no basis for disagreement.

712 Someone told me one day that he felt full of joy and confidence when he had been to confession. Someone else told me that he was still afraid. My reaction was that one good man could be made by putting these two together, for each of them lacked something in not sharing the feelings of the other. The same thing often happens in other connexions.

739 Truth is so obscured nowadays and lies so well established that unless we love the truth we shall never recognize it.

740 Weaklings are those who know the truth, but maintain it only as far as it is in their interest to do so, and apart from that forsake it.

741 The adding-machine produces effects closer to thought than anything done by the animals, but it does nothing to justify the assertion that it has a will like the animals.

742 Even if people's interests are not affected by what they say, it must not be definitely concluded that they are not lying for there are some people who lie simply for the sake of lying.

743 There is some pleasure in being on board a ship battered by storms when one is certain of not perishing. The persecutions buffeting the Church are like this.

744 When we do not know the truth about something, it is a good thing that there should be some common error on which men's minds can fix, as, for example, the attribution to the moon of changes of seasons, progress of diseases, etc. For man's chief malady is restless curiosity about things he cannot know, and it is not so bad for him to be wrong as so vainly curious.

746 On the fact that neither Josephus, nor Tacitus, nor other historians, spoke of Jesus Christ.

Far from telling against him, this is on the contrary in his favour. For it is certain that Jesus Christ existed, that his religion made a great stir, and so it is obvious that they simply concealed it on purpose, or that they spoke about it and that it was suppressed or changed.

749 How warped is the judgement by which there is nobody who does not put himself above the rest of the world, and who does not prefer his own good, and continuing happiness and survival to that of the rest of the world!

750 Cromwell was about to ravage the whole of Christendom; the royal family was lost and his own set for ever in power, but for a little grain of sand getting into his bladder. Even Rome was about to tremble beneath him. But, with this bit of gravel once there, he died, his family fell into disgrace, peace reigned and the king was restored.

751 Those who are accustomed to judge by feeling have no understanding of matters involving reasoning. For they want to go right to the bottom of things at a glance, and are not accustomed to look for principles. The others, on the contrary, who are accustomed to reason from principles, have no understanding of matters involving feeling, because they look for principles and are unable to see things at a glance.

752 Two sorts of people make everything equal, for example holidays and working days, Christians and

priests, all the sins amongst themselves. And from this some people conclude that what is bad for priests is also bad for Christians, while others conclude that what is not bad for Christians is permissible for priests.

753 When Augustus learned that among the children under two put to death by Herod was his own son, he said that it was better to be Herod's pig than his son. (Macrobius, *Saturnalia*, lib. ii, ch. iv.)

754 First degree: to be blamed for doing badly or praised for doing well.

Second degree: to be neither praised nor blamed.

755 *He maketh a vain god.*

Disgust.

756 *Thought.* All man's dignity consists in thought, but what is this thought? How silly it is!

Thought, then, is admirable and incomparable by its very nature. It must have had strange faults to have become worthy of contempt, but it does have such faults that nothing is more ridiculous. How great it is by its nature, how vile by its faults!

757 *Draining away.* It is an appalling thing to feel all one possesses drain away.

758 *Light. Darkness.* There would be too much darkness if there were no visible signs of the truth. One admirable sign of it is that it has always resided in a visible Church and congregation. There would be too much light if there were only one opinion in

the Church. That which has always existed is the true one, for the true one has always been there, but no false one has always been there.

759 Thought constitutes man's greatness.

764 All the major forms of diversion are dangerous for the Christian life, but among all those which the world has invented none is more to be feared than the theatre. It represents passions so naturally and delicately that it arouses and engenders them in our heart, especially that of love; above all when it is represented as very chaste and virtuous. For the more innocent it seems to innocent souls, the more liable they are to be touched by it; its violence appeals to our self-esteem, which at once conceives the desire to produce the same effects which we see so well represented. At the same time our conscience is conditioned by the irreproachable sentiments to be seen there, which remove the fear of pure souls, who imagine that purity is not offended by loving with a love which seems to them so prudent.

Thus we leave the theatre with hearts so full of all the beauty and sweetness of love, and our mind so convinced of its innocence, that we are quite prepared to receive our first impressions of it, or rather to seek the opportunity of arousing them in someone else's heart, so that we may enjoy the same pleasures and sacrifices as those which we have seen so well depicted in the theatre.

765 If lightning struck low-lying places, etc., poets and people who can only argue about things of this kind would be without proofs.

767 As the ranks of duke, king and magistrate are real and necessary (because power governs all things) they exist at all times and in all places, but, since it is mere whim that makes it this or that person, there is no consistency about it, it is liable to variation, etc.

768 The commands of reason are much more imperative than those of any master, for if we disobey the one we are unhappy, but if we disobey the other we are foolish.

773 Only the contest appeals to us, not the victory.

We like to watch animals fighting, but not the victor falling upon the vanquished. What did we want to see but the final victory? And once it has happened we have had enough. It is the same with gaming, with the pursuit of truth. We like to see the clash of opinions in debate, but do we want to contemplate the truth once it is found? Not at all. If we are to enjoy it, we must see it arising from the debate. It is the same with passions; there is some pleasure in seeing the collision of two opposites, but when one asserts its mastery it becomes mere brutality.

We never go after things in themselves, but the pursuit of things. Thus in the theatre scenes of unclouded happiness are no good, any more than extreme and hopeless misery, or brutal love affairs, or harsh cruelty.

802 Time heals pain and quarrels because we change. We are no longer the same persons; neither the offender nor the offended are themselves any more. It is as if one angered a nation and came back to see them after two generations. They are still Frenchmen, but not the same ones.

803 If we dreamed the same thing every night, it would affect us as much as the objects we see every day. And if an artisan was sure of dreaming for twelve hours every night that he was king, I believe he would be almost as happy as a king who dreamed for twelve hours every night that he was an artisan.

If we dreamed every night that we were being pursued by enemies and troubled by these distressing apparitions, and spent every day doing something different, as one does on a journey, we should suffer almost as much as if it were true, and would dread going to sleep as we dread waking up when we are afraid of really encountering some misfortune. And this would in fact cause almost as much pain as reality.

But because dreams are all different, and there is variety even within each one, what we see in them affects us much less than what we see when we are awake, because of the continuity. This, however, is not so continuous and even that it does not change too, though less abruptly, except on rare occasions, as on a journey, when we say: 'It seems like a dream.' For life is a dream, but somewhat less changeable.

804 Are we to say that men recognized original sin because they said that justice had left the earth? *Call no man happy until he is dead*. Does that mean that they knew that eternal and absolute happiness begins at death?

805 By knowing each man's ruling passion, we can be sure of pleasing him, and yet each has fancies contrary to his own good, in the very idea he has of good, and this oddity is disconcerting.

806 We are not satisfied with the life we have in ourselves and our own being. We want to lead an imaginary life in the eyes of others, and so we try to make an impression. We strive constantly to embellish and preserve our imaginary being, and neglect the real one. And if we are calm, or generous, or loyal, we are anxious to have it known so that we can attach these virtues to our other existence; we prefer to detach them from our real self so as to unite them with the other. We would cheerfully be cowards if that would acquire us a reputation for bravery. How clear a sign of the nullity of our own being that we are not satisfied with one without the other and often exchange one for the other! For anyone who would not die to save his honour would be infamous.

808 There are three ways to believe: reason, habit, inspiration. Christianity, which alone has reason,

does not admit as its true children those who believe without inspiration. It is not that it excludes reason and habit, quite the contrary, but we must open our mind to the proofs, confirm ourselves in it through habit, while offering ourselves through humiliations to inspiration, which alone can produce the real and salutary effect. *Lest the Cross of Christ be made of none effect.*

812 The style of the Gospels is remarkable in so many ways; among others for never putting in any invective against the executioners and enemies of Christ. For there is none in any of the historians against Judas, Pilate or any of the Jews.

If this restraint of the Evangelists had been put on, together with many other features of such fine character, and if they had only put it on in order to draw attention to it, not daring to remark on it themselves, they would not have failed to acquire friends to make such remarks for their benefit. But, since they acted as they did without affectation and quite disinterestedly, they did not cause anyone to remark on it. And I believe that many of these things have never been remarked on before. That shows how coolly the thing was done.

813 We never do evil so fully and cheerfully as when we do it out of conscience.

814 We pervert our feelings just as we pervert our minds.

Our minds and feelings are trained by the company we keep, and perverted by the company we keep. Thus good or bad company trains or perverts respectively. It is therefore very important to be able to make the right choice so that we train rather than pervert. And we cannot make this choice unless it is already trained, and not perverted. This is thus a vicious circle from which anyone is lucky to escape.

815 Ordinary people have the ability not to think about things they do not want to think about. 'Do not think about the passages concerning the Messiah,' said the Jew to his son. Our own people often behave like this, and this is how false religions are preserved, and even the true one as far as many people are concerned.

But there are some without this ability to stop themselves thinking, who think all the more for being forbidden to do so. These people rid themselves of false religions, and even of the true one, unless they find solid arguments for them.

816 'I should soon have given up a life of pleasure,' they say, 'if I had faith.' But I tell you: 'You would soon have faith if you gave up a life of pleasure. Now it is up to you to begin. If I could give you faith, I would. But I cannot, nor can I test the truth of what you say, but you can easily give up your pleasure and test whether I am telling the truth.'

817 There is no denying it; one must admit that there is something astonishing about Christianity. 'It is

because you were born in it,' they will say. Far from it; I stiffen myself against it for that very reason, for fear of being corrupted by prejudice. But, though I was born in it, I cannot help finding it astonishing.

937 When our passions impel us to do something we forget our duty. For example, if we like a book, we read it when we ought to be doing something else. But to remember our duty we need only decide to do something we dislike; we then make the excuse of something else to be done, and thus remember our duty.

938 The figure used in the Gospel for the state of the soul that is sick is that of sick bodies. But, because one body cannot be sick enough to express it properly, there had to be more than one. Thus we find the deaf man, the dumb man, the blind man, the paralytic, dead Lazarus, the man possessed of a devil. All these put together are in the sick soul.

939 'The servant knoweth not what his lord doeth,' because the lord only tells him what to do and not the purpose of it. That is why he obeys slavishly and often sins against the purpose. But Jesus Christ has told us the purpose.

And you destroy that purpose.

940 Jesus did not want to be killed without the forms of justice, for it is much more ignominious to die at the hands of justice than in some unjust insurrection.

THE STORY OF PENGUIN CLASSICS

Before 1946 ... 'Classics' are mainly the domain of academics and students; readable editions for everyone else are almost unheard of. This all changes when a little-known classicist, E. V. Rieu, presents Penguin founder Allen Lane with the translation of Homer's *Odyssey* that he has been working on in his spare time.

1946 Penguin Classics debuts with *The Odyssey*, which promptly sells three million copies. Suddenly, classics are no longer for the privileged few.

1950s Rieu, now series editor, turns to professional writers for the best modern, readable translations, including Dorothy L. Sayers's *Inferno* and Robert Graves's unexpurgated *Twelve Caesars*.

1960s The Classics are given the distinctive black covers that have remained a constant throughout the life of the series. Rieu retires in 1964, hailing the Penguin Classics list as 'the greatest educative force of the twentieth century.'

1970s A new generation of translators swells the Penguin Classics ranks, introducing readers of English to classics of world literature from more than twenty languages. The list grows to encompass more history, philosophy, science, religion and politics.

1980s The Penguin American Library launches with titles such as *Uncle Tom's Cabin*, and joins forces with Penguin Classics to provide the most comprehensive library of world literature available from any paperback publisher.

1990s The launch of Penguin Audiobooks brings the classics to a listening audience for the first time, and in 1999 the worldwide launch of the Penguin Classics website extends their reach to the global online community.

The 21st Century Penguin Classics are completely redesigned for the first time in nearly twenty years. This world-famous series now consists of more than 1300 titles, making the widest range of the best books ever written available to millions – and constantly redefining what makes a 'classic'.

The Odyssey continues ...

The best books ever written

PENGUIN 🐧 CLASSICS

SINCE 1946

Find out more at www.penguinclassics.com